A Blueprint for Literacy Success

Building a Foundation for Beginning Readers and Writers

Sandra Iversen

ACKNOWLEDGEMENT

Lands End wishes to thank Target Road School, Glenfield, Auckland, New Zealand, for their generosity and co-operation. In particular, we wish to thank teachers Tracey Reeder and Paul Reeder and their students who agreed to be photographed for this book.

Contents

Introduction   5

1 Mastering the Terminology   7

Letter-Sound Recognition   7
Cues   8
Decontextualized Language   8
Listening Comprehension   8
Metacognition/Metacognitive
     Awareness   9
Onsets and Rimes   9
Orthographic Analogies   9
Phonemes   10
Phonological/Phonemic Awareness   10
Phonics   10
Strategies   11

2 Beginning with Letter-Sound Recognition   13

Heavy-Duty Letters   14
Teaching Letters   15

3 Introducing New Words   23

Exploring Word Meanings
    ----Learning New Vocabulary   24
Increasing Children's Vocabulary   25
Increasing Recognition
     of Words in Print   32

4 Getting Under Way with Writing   43

Six Guidelines for Writing   43
Strategies for Early Writing   46
Teaching Children How to Hear and
     Record Sounds   48
Using the Elkonin Boxes   52
Learning High-Frequency Words   54
Using Orthographic Analogies   58
Helping Children Compose Messages   63
Exploring Shared Experiences   63
Ideas for Shared Experiences   63

5 Choosing and Using Little Books   69

Grouping Children for
     Instructional Reading   70
Choosing Instructional Reading
     Material for Beginning Readers   70
Introducing and Reading
     the First Little Books   71

6 Putting It All Together   75

Assess Exactly What Each Child Can Do   76
Design Learning Experiences Based on
     What the Children Already Know   77
Help Children Succeed in Their Attempts   78
Evaluate Progress   80

Blackline Masters   81

References   125

Index   126

Introduction

> *"I've got a class of children just starting school. We aren't in a very affluent area and lots of our children don't speak English very well. What I want to know right now is how to get all my kids reading and writing as quickly as possible."*

A Blueprint for Literacy Success is designed to answer some common questions about beginning literacy and to make your teaching life a bit easier. As teachers, you are most aware of the great responsibility that lies on your shoulders. It is important to get all children off to a good start.

The research into early literacy consistently tells us that those children who do not make good progress after a year of instruction continue to fall further behind their age peers. Instead of being able to learn more about reading and writing every time they read and write, these children soon meet material that is too hard.

The children's lack of reading expertise soon gets in the way of their learning subject content knowledge across other curriculum areas. Soon those children not making good progress in reading and writing start to lose confidence in themselves as well, which can lead to negative self-images.

Children come to school with different amounts of literacy knowledge and different cultural literacy practices. They also make different rates of progress when they get to school. However, because we want all our children to be successful in our market-driven western society, we know it is important that they all be competent and fluent in reading, writing and speaking English.

A Blueprint for Literacy Success can help you help your students achieve that competency. This book gives you lots of practical teaching ideas for your classroom that are based on the latest research into beginning reading and writing, and will help you understand why these ideas work. By understanding why the ideas work, you will be able to come up with your own ideas for your classroom. Also suggested are worthwhile activities that the children can work on independently. They can do these alone, with a friend, or in a small group, which will give you more quality time teaching others.

A Blueprint for Literacy Success contains chapters on some important aspects of early literacy learning.

CHAPTER 1 defines some of the terminology that is currently appearing in the literacy literature. Understanding these terms can help avoid confusion and allow you to realize that new terminology is often a refinement and an extension of familiar terms and concepts.

CHAPTER 2 addresses those aspects of teaching concerned with alphabet letter names and sounds. There is currently much debate in the literacy literature about whether to teach letter sounds systematically or whether children pick them up incidentally. This chapter contends that children must learn letter names and sounds if they are to read and write using an alphabetic script. It suggests that some letters are more useful than others to children beginning reading and writing and that these should be taught first. Also contained in this chapter are many suggestions for teaching letter names and sounds that arise from authentic contexts within the course of the school day.

CHAPTER 3 suggests that for young children there are two aspects to learning new words. The first is expanding vocabulary or understanding word meanings, and the second, recognizing words in print. Children must understand words and have them in their listening vocabulary before they meet them in reading.

Children who have had numerous stories read to them in their early years have had many opportunities to increase their vocabulary. These children have a distinct advantage over those children who have not been exposed to reading in the preschool years. This chapter provides models for teaching both vocabulary and word recognition.

CHAPTER 4 addresses beginning writing. It suggests six guidelines for getting children off to a good start in writing. There are many practical suggestions for teaching early writing strategies and for motivating children to write beyond their own personal experiences.

CHAPTER 5 gives some insights into how to scaffold the reading task so that children can read books on their own without having had them previously read aloud to them. During this instructional, or guided, reading time you should be able to see which skills and strategies the children control when they are working independently at a reading task that requires some problem solving. Choosing and introducing material appropriately is discussed.

CHAPTER 6 suggests some powerful teaching methods that quickly help children become readers and writers. Also included at the back of the book are a variety of blackline masters for your use in implementing many of the teaching strategies suggested here.

1
Mastering the Terminology

> *"Could you please explain some of those terms that we hear all the time now?"*

Familiarity with current literacy terminology and concepts will help you define what you do in your classroom and give you a means of communicating about your practice without confusion. You will also get more from the journal articles you read and find conference presentations easier to understand, and a working knowledge of terms helps you keep up-to-date with current research.

You will probably find that many of the terms apply to concepts with which you are already familiar.

Letter-Sound Recognition

Letter-Sound Recognition refers to the names and sounds of alphabet letters, and the relationship between the two. Children using an alphabetic reading and writing system must become conceptually aware that there is a code to be deciphered.

Knowledge of the names of alphabet letters, though not a cause of being able to read, is a reliable predictor of beginning reading achievement, probably because many letter names also contain their sound. A child's ability to use letter-sound / sound-letter relationships is crucial to acquiring reading and writing.

Cues

Cue use helps readers identify words that are not readily recognized. Three cues are available for children to use when beginning reading. Semantic or meaning cues, syntactic or language structure cues, and graphophonic cues which relate to phonemes, the sound of language.

Semantic cues are accessed through the story and the pictures and through the child's prior knowledge.

Syntactic cues are accessed through the readers's oral language and knowledge of book language and English grammatical patterns.

Graphophonic cues are accessed through the child's alphabet letter knowledge and letter-sound recognition.

Distinctive patterns of cue use can be detected in children's beginning reading and are often a reflection of the teaching methodology employed. The goal of beginning reading is for children to use all the cues in concert to help them comprehend what is being read.

Decontextualized Language

If children are able to describe a situation so that someone else can understand it without being present at the event, they are said to be able to use decontextualized language.

Compare

"He hit him here see," with "Jed punched Mike on the back."

Books are written in decontextualized form. To be able to use oral language for predicting text while reading, children need to be able to use decontextualized language in their everyday speech.

Listening Comprehension

Listening comprehension refers to the children's understanding of text when it is read to them.

Reading may be said to be a combination of listening comprehension and decoding. If the children can decode all the words in a passage but not understand the message, they are not reading. Likewise, if children can understand when something is read to them but cannot decode the words independently, they are not reading.

Listening comprehension is important to beginning reading because it is while listening to stories that children learn book language, book structure, new concepts and new vocabulary. All these then become part of the prior knowledge that the children can bring to the reading task.

Metacognition/ Metacognitive Awareness

Related to reading, metacognition or meta-cognitive awareness refers to the ability of the reader to monitor his or her own reading comprehensiona and alter reading strategies accordingly.

Metacognitive strategies----that is, knowing how, when and where to use infor-mation, rather than just items of knowledge----are important in reading and writing ac-quisition because they lead to independence.

Onsets and Rimes

Young children can more easily identify an intermediate level of word segmentation that divides words into units that are smaller than syllables, but bigger than phonemes (see discussion below). These units are called onsets and rimes (Treiman, 1992).

The onset is the letter or letter cluster that precedes the vowel in a monosyllabic word, and the rime is the vowel and any subsequent consonants. For example, in the word *wing, w* is the onset and *ing* is the rime. Often the rime is, in fact, the rhyming segment of the words such as in *wing, sing,* and *ring.*

The ability to use onsets and rimes helps with both spelling and word identification. Although the English language is often said to be irregular, there are thirty-five dependable rimes, that is, rimes whose pronunciation doesn't change, regardless of the onset. From these consistent endings, nearly five hundred words can be made. Some examples of dependable rimes are: *ail, ack, ide, ight, ole, op, ug* and *unk (*Wylie and Durrell, 1970).

For a complete list see "Thirty-Five Dependable Rimes" on page 47.

Orthographic Analogies

Even very young children are able to make analogies. Orthographic analogies refer to the word families that can be generated from knowing beginning letters / letter clusters (onsets) and rhymes (rimes).

By using orthographic analogies, children can quickly increase their reading and writing vocabularies. Being able to make analogies also helps the children solve unknown words in reading and generate new words in writing. For example, the child who knows the word *cat* can use a rime analogy to read or write any word that rhymes with *cat,* for example *fat, bat* and *hat.*

Phonemes

Phonemes are the smallest units of sound in a word. For example, the word *boat* has three phonemes: */b/, /oa/, /t/.*

Phonemes are very important to beginning reading and writing. When children invent their spellings in writing, they use phonemes and alphabet letters. In effect, they are segmenting the word they want to write into its constituent sounds and then writing the corresponding letters. For example, a beginning writer might write *bot* for *boat.*

Working on these sound-letter correspondences helps with the visual discrimination of letters needed in reading.

Phonological/ Phonemic Awareness

Phonemic and phonological awareness refers to a variety of tasks related to the sounds of language. These tasks have different levels of difficulty. Beginning readers and writers need to be able to perform the following phonological tasks:

- Distinguish words that rhyme from words that don't rhyme.
  "Tell me which words sound the same: **cat, pig, hat**."

- Distinguish words that start or end the same from words that don't. *"Tell me which words start the same*: **pig, pen, horse**."

- Match sound to sound.
  "Is there a **t** *in* **hat**?"

- Segment words into sounds.
  "Tell me the sounds in **cat**."

- Blend sounds into words.
  "Tell me what this word is /**c**/, /**a**/, /**t**/."

- Invent spelling.

Research into reading difficulties shows that phonemic awareness deficiency is a major cause of reading disability. Many research studies have also shown that phonemic awareness tasks can be successfully taught to very young children and that this knowledge greatly assists with both reading and writing acquisition.

Phonics

Phonics is a method of teaching reading, especially beginning reading, that stresses the systematic acquisition of sound-symbol relationships.

Also associated with this method of teaching are reading books designed to reflect the sounds being taught. Children often follow the instructional sequence of the lesson with a worksheet activity.

Strategies

Strategies are a bit like understanding, not visible and hard to measure, but indicative of what a child can do in a certain situation. For example, you can say a child has strategies for getting to unknown words in writing if he or she sounds the word out, asks someone, copies the word from somewhere, uses a rime analogy or knows how to write the word correctly. One important reading strategy is knowing how to search for and use cues to monitor ongoing reading comprehension.

Using strategies rather than items of knowledge is important in reading and writing acquisition because it leads to independence. Once children know how to use appropriate strategies in their reading and writing, they are able to learn a little more about reading and writing every time they read and write.

Researchers and educators are making great leaps in knowledge and the more they learn, the more the vocabulary will grow to keep up with it. It is not important to be able to recite the definitions verbatim or that you know every new buzz word in education. However, it is important that you know the concepts driving educational research so that you can be the best teacher you can be.

2
Beginning with Letter-Sound Recognition

"How important is the alphabet?"

"Won't children just pick up the letter names and sounds during the course of their language experiences?"

All children need to know the relationship between letter names and letter sounds, that is, graphemes and phonemes. They also need to know how to use this information in reading and writing to solve and spell new words and to check that what they have read or written is correct.

Teachers have many different ways of teaching the alphabet letters, some more formal than others. Some teachers start with the letter *a*, and go through the alphabet, one letter name a week to *z*. Other teachers do likewise but teach only the letter sound. Some teachers teach letter names, one a week, and letter sounds following strict phonic rules. Still other teachers combine letter name and letter-sound learning with the teaching of handwriting and group those letters together with similar formation patterns, such as, *o, a, d, g.*

We have found that teaching a few heavy-duty letters is the most effective way of teaching beginning letter-sound relationships. Teaching a few letters explicitly and asking the children to use this knowledge in their reading and writing helps children not only learn some letters but learn a purpose for learning letters.

Heavy-Duty Letters

To get children to use their knowledge of alphabet letters in their reading and writing, start by teaching those heavy-duty letters that often begin the words
in the children's little readers and start words that children like to write.

These letters are

Ss Mm Bb Hh Tt Rr

Ff Cc Ww Pp Ll

These consonants are useful to learn first because

- They don't look alike, so they will not be confusing. Many children take a while to sort out similar looking letters. Trying to teach *b* and *d* a week apart may only add to the confusion.

- Children can use the sounds to help them predict and check their reading.

- They are useful letters for the children to use in their writing.

- They often begin the words that children will encounter in their first reading books. An investigation of over 100 beginning reading books shows the occurrence of the following high-frequency reading and high-interest words.

High-Frequency Words

said see
make made me more my
big by but because
had has have he her here him
to
ready run ran
for from
can come came coming
can't could cannot
we when with will where went
want was would what were
put
like little look looking let

High-Interest Words

soft slow sister
mum monkey Monday
baby brother black blue
happy hard hot
today teddy ten Tuesday town
rabbit red
fall fell fast fish
cat car
winter wind water wet white
please pen puppy pink play
lion letter

It will not be necessary to explicitly teach any letters besides the heavy-duty letters to most children. By the time they have learned the upper– and lower-case versions of the eleven heavy-duty letters and have learned how to use them in their daily reading and writing, most children will be able to learn the rest of the letters incidentally. You should remember, though, that there will be a small group of children who will require further explicit teaching of the letter names and sounds. You will be quickly able to identify those children.

They may be those who

- Came to school with little or no knowledge of alphabet names.
- Pay little attention during your teaching of the alphabet letters.
- Do not remember the letters that you have taught.
- Are unable to write their own name or any letters in their name.

Teaching Letters

It is important to make many opportunities for letter-learning during the course of the school day. You can teach letters while you demonstrate, while you question and provide contexts for children to problem solve, and during independent practice time. You may want to encourage the children to try some of the following activities.

- **CREATE** a letter book.

- **CREATE** a wall frieze.

- **SOLVE** language riddles:

  "I'm thinking of a word
  that starts with **w.**
  It's what I swim in at the beach.
  It's called the _____."

- **ENCOURAGE** the children to help you write the **Daily News.**

Daily News is a good time to explore words that start with a focus letter and to demonstrate spelling techniques.

- **PLAY** games.

Daily News

Today is windy Wednesday.
Today is wet Wednesday.

Which words start with W
or w?

  windy
  Wednesday
  wet
  Which
  words
  with

we   water   wool   witch   wink
William   wind   win   window

For example, you may use a feely bag full of common objects such as a pencil, boat, fork and spoon.

Have each child pull out an object, say what it is, and say another word that starts the same way.

- **USE** plastic or magnetic letters or letter cards to answer riddles.

*"Who can bring me all the **m**'s?*
*All the letters that make the **m** sound?"*

- **IDENTIFY** letters after the reading of big books, songs and poems.

*"Who can use the pointer to show me a word starting with **m**?"*

- **ANSWER** questions during shared writing.

"What can you hear at the end of ___?"
"What letter will I need to write?"

- **EXTEND** their knowledge during guided writing.

Group together three or four children who have demonstrated some ability in hearing sounds. Ask them questions similar to those in the shared writing example to help them write as independently as possible. Use this time to focus on specific instruction or problems the child is having.

- **USE** free time for independent practice.

- **MAKE** a letter chart or a letter book.

- **MATCH** the initial letters with the pictures.

- **MATCH** upper- and lower-case letters using the letter cards, magnetic letters or letters cut from magazines.

- **FIND** words that start with the same given letter.

- **USE** illustrations or magazine pictures to make a letter montage.

- **SORT** pictures of objects starting with the same letter.

- **READ** poems containing heavy-duty letters.

You may want to use Blackline Masters 11-43 in the independent reading centre.

Tt

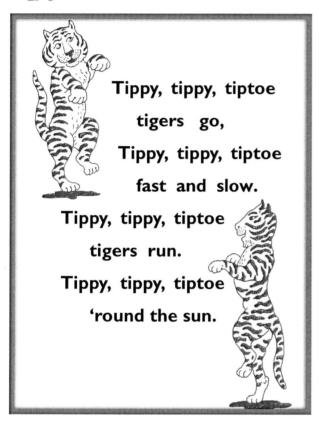

Tippy, tippy, tiptoe
tigers go,
Tippy, tippy, tiptoe
fast and slow.
Tippy, tippy, tiptoe
tigers run.
Tippy, tippy, tiptoe
'round the sun.

Ll

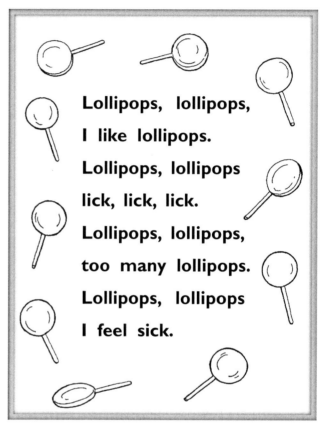

Lollipops, lollipops,
I like lollipops.
Lollipops, lollipops
lick, lick, lick.
Lollipops, lollipops,
too many lollipops.
Lollipops, lollipops
I feel sick.

When children are just beginning to read or write, they will need to learn the most important letters first. Explicit teaching of the heavy-duty letters will give your students a strong foundation to build on. Once they have learned the heavy-duty letters, they will be better prepared to learn the rest of the alphabet with less explicit instruction.

3
Introducing New Words

*"How important is it for children
to learn new words?"*

*"Will they just pick them up incidentally
or should they be taught?"*

*"Are some ways of teaching words
better than others?"*

In order to become fluent readers, children must learn new words. Some teachers following strict phonics programmes believe that children should learn words before they even begin to read books for themselves. Other teachers believe that children will acquire new vocabulary naturally in the course of being exposed to print. There are elements of truth in each of these points of view.

In essence, there are two separate elements that are necessary to "learn new words": understanding word meaning (vocabulary), and recognising words in print (word recognition). Both these elements are integral parts of reading.

Exploring Word Meanings-Learning New Vocabulary

Research into increasing vocabulary shows that children best learn new word meanings by hearing and seeing them in authentic and meaningful contexts (Elley,1989; Mason, 1992). The two best places for this to occur are during a read-aloud to children and during the free reading that children do for themselves. Children who have had many stories read to them before they go to school are much more prepared for learning to read. This is because they have had many opportunities to meet new words and ideas, and these words have become part of their listening comprehension. As familiarity with new vocabulary grows, children start to use these words in their oral language.

Mark, age three, was helping his father in the garden. They were wheelbarrowing soil to make a new garden. Mark had his own little wheel barrow. As the pile of soil for the new garden got bigger, Mark said to his dad, *"It's virtually impossible for me to tip this on top."*

Kimberly, age four, was looking out the car window. She saw where someone had thrown soft drink cans onto the side of the road. She said, *"Look Mum. That's pollution!"*

The following flow chart shows the process of new vocabulary acquisition.

Reading aloud to children and independent reading by children introduces new words and ideas

New words and ideas become familiar and become part of children's listening comprehension

These words and their meanings become part of the prior knowledge that children bring to their reading

Children start to experiment and use those new words in their oral language

Increasing Children's Vocabulary

Try the following activities to help your students increase their vocabulary knowledge.

• **READ** a variety of different text types to children every single day. Read new books and old favourites.

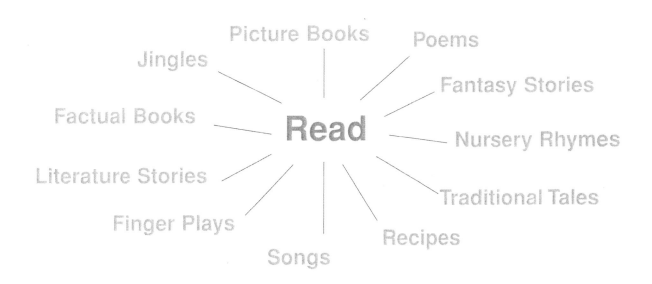

- **EXPLAIN** and expand on vocabulary and concepts where necessary without killing the story. Children will learn new vocabulary without this, but doing it occasionally will help.

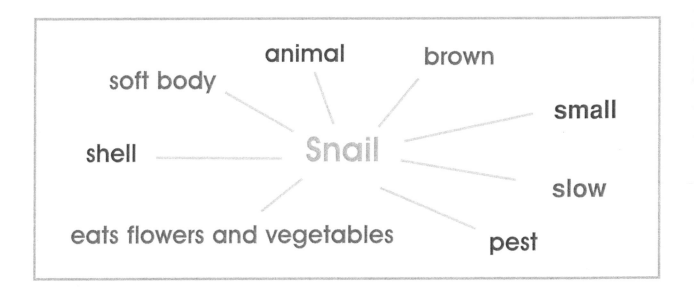

- **Make** and display word maps with the children. These maps are designed to expand the children's vocabulary and knowledge about certain items or objects. Always use a word that appears in the book you have just read.

- **Make** and display word steps with the children using a word from the book you have just read.

Start with a word such as *boiling*. Ask children for a word that means the opposite.

-Write one of these words at the top of the steps and the other at the bottom.
-Then ask the children for the words that might fit in between.

To begin, very young children will need a lot of help from you to do this. It is quite all right for you to suggest the words. The objective of the activity is that children add to their vocabularies.

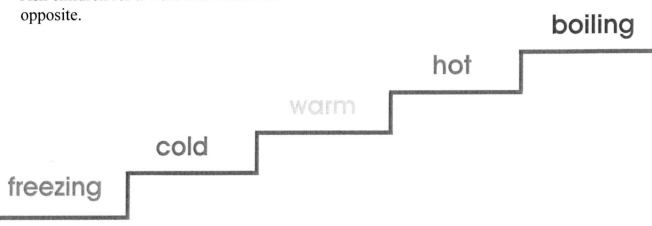

- **EXPAND** understandings through concrete language experiences.

-Use the adventure playground or physical education equipment to explain basic spatial concepts. Jump *through* the tyres, climb *over* the bench, crawl *under* the swing.

-Have the children use hula hoops to

Make a shape with their legs **outside** *the hoop and the rest of the body* **inside.**

Make a shape with only one arm **inside** *the hoop.*

Make a shape with the hoop **behind** *the head.*

Record the experience for the children to illustrate and display this as a wall story. (See "The Cycle of the Wall Story" on page 29 for details.)

> *We went outside with the hula hoops.*
>
> *We made shapes with our legs outside the hula hoop.*
>
> *We made shapes with one arm inside the hula hoop.*
>
> *We made shapes with the hula hoop behind our heads.*

We made a shape with our legs outside the hula hoop.

We made a shape with one arm inside the hula hoop.

- **SHARE** books with children and then innovate on predictable language patterns. Display and use these stories in the same way as the language experience stories.

Brontosaurus was a big dinosaur. It had a body bigger than the school!

Bodie.

Pterodactylus was a flying dinosaur. It had wings and claws.

Maria

1. Allosaurus

Allosaurus was a big dinosaur. It had sharp teeth and strong back legs with large, sharp claws. Allosaurus ate other dinosaurs.

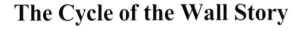

The Cycle of the Wall Story

Wall stories are a very good way of increasing the amount of reading material available to children in your class. If you display the story on the wall, or attached to wire across the room, you increase the number of children who can read it at the same time.

1. Provide the experience or model for the innovation.

2. Work with the children to formulate the text. Make sure it is simple and readable for your class.

3. Write the text in large print on separate pages.

4. Provide the children with appropriate size paper for the illustrations. Make sure they know

5. Decide the medium for the illustrations. Crayon-and-dye is easy and colourful. If there are many children involved you may ask them to work in pairs or ask children to colour and cut out part of the illustration. These can be pasted on the page later. Be sure to make a note of which children are illustrating what. Little children can often forget what they have offered to do.

6. Assemble the wall story by pasting the text and the illustration on brown paper backing.

7. Attach the story to the wall or a wire at a height that the children can read.

8. Read the completed text as a class as a shared reading and individually during free reading time.

9. When the text is familiar-at the end of a week-fold it and staple it into a big book. Use it as independent reading.

10. Replace it with a new story.

MAKE time each day for free, independent reading. To start, very young children will be looking at books or telling the story rather than reading. Although they are not reading, the expectation is important.

- Start the first week of school.

- Expect that children will read independently every single day.

- Set aside a time for this free reading – right after recess or lunch is often appropriate.

- Start with five minutes a day.

- Gradually increase the time to

  - 15 minutes for first year at school;
  - 20 minutes daily for second year;
  - 30 minutes daily for third year.

You may wish to formalize this free reading time into SSR (sustained silent reading) or DEAR (drop everything and read).

Procedures for SSR and DEAR

- Have each child choose a book or books before the session begins. You may need to provide some guidance with this early in the year. Do not allow children to move around once the session has started.

- Start with five minutes and gradually increase the time as for free reading.

- Model the importance of reading by reading yourself during this time.

- Enlist school support to ensure that there are no interruptions during this time.

Free reading may be reading

instructional reading books	children's published writing
charts	the computer
overhead transparencies	big books
stories	poems
songs	at the listening post
story books	topic books

Increasing Recognition of Words in Print

Children learn to recognize new words by seeing them over and over in different contexts. The words then become part of the child's visual memory, that is, the child is able to decode them. The following suggestions can help you create an environment that helps your students increase their word recognition.

- **PROVIDE** a print-saturated environment where words appear in context.

- **USE** simple statements and questions to label the environment.

Which activity will you choose?

Put your home reader here.

Can you draw this flower?

This is the poem box.

Have you signed in today?

What is the weather like today?

The scissors are kept here.

Science alive!

Come here and read a book.

- **LABEL** co-operative art work and display this on the walls at a height at which children can read.

- **KEEP** poems, charts, songs and big books accessible. Keep these available for independent reading.

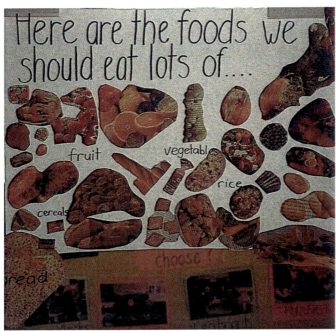

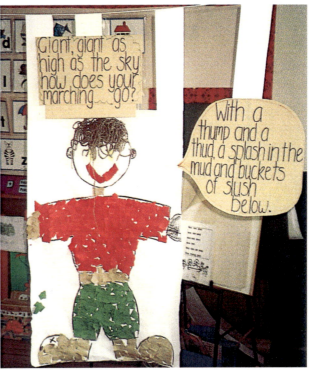

An example of *Daily News* for Monday

> ***Today is Monday.***
>
> ***Michael came to school today.***
>
> ***It is Michael's birthday. He is five today.***
>
> ***Michael got a toy car for his birthday.***
>
> ***Today it is Mr Reeder's birthday too.***
>
> ***Mrs Reeder gave him a puppy for his birthday.***
>
> ***Mr Reeder likes his puppy.***
>
> ***He is going to call him Nelson.***

- **MAKE** at least one new wall story each week that incorporates the short high-frequency words that you want the children to learn. This may be the same story that you used to expand vocabulary, or it may be different. Use language experiences that the children have participated in and innovations on books that you have read with the children in shared and guided situations.

- **RECORD** class news daily. Keep the class news, or Daily News, each day. At the end of each week staple the five sheets together and hang them in an accessible place for reference. Encourage children to revisit these news books as part of free reading. The Daily News also may be illustrated.

- **ENSURE** that there are many opportunities for teaching and learning short high-frequency words. There are 70 words that children find easiest to learn, and they form a valuable bank of known words.

This list of 70 words was compiled from the results of testing one hundred children with the Dolch Word List. The list is in order, starting from the word that most of the children identified (Iversen, 1994).

up	we	a	and	go	I	in	the
to	you	for	red	he	too	look	
one	me	see	my	it	can	is	at
come	into	like	big	blue	all		
are	down	not	she	little	yellow		
said	no	be	so	am	on	out	
an	did	get	away	but	have		
by	that	going	make	yes	here		
this	will	of	they	had	then		
was	his	went	at	are	it	by	
came	with	little					

• **ASK** children to locate the new high-frequency word in a text after they have read the story. You may also revise previously learned words in the same way.

For example, after guided reading with individual little books you may say,
  *"Turn to page 3/ Show me **up.***
  *Find **up** on the next page.*
  *Who can find **up** on the last page?"*

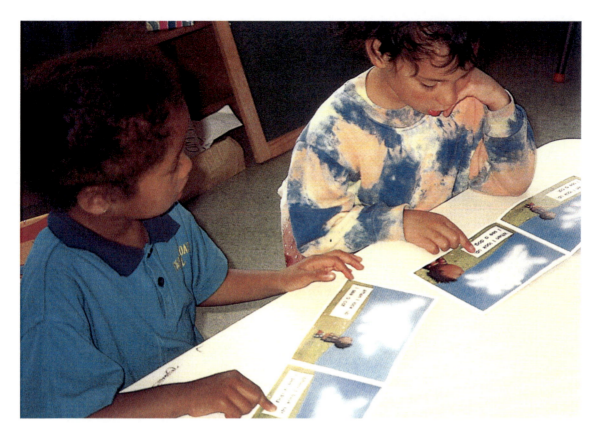

If children are unsure, have them check their responses by rereading the page while finger pointing.

During shared reading with a big book, you may say,

*"Who can come and show all the children the word **and**? Is she right?"*

*"Who can come and find **and** again on this page? Is he right?"*

"What does this word say?"

• **SHARE** poems, songs and big books, that contain short high-frequency words.

• **USE** the rhyming jingles that follow to focus on particular sight words. Photocopy the Blackline Masters 11-43 in the back of this book and introduce them as a shared reading with the entire class or group. Copy one for each child. Have each child paste it into their own blank Jingle Book to illustrate and read independently. Place your jingle in a Jingle Box for free reading. Introduce a new jingle every two or three days.

Away, went, the, to, on, his

Away went the cat.
Away went the dog.
Away went the frog
to sit on his log.

One, yellow, up, the, was, by, me

One yellow bird
flew up in the tree.
One yellow banana
was eaten by me!

I, like

I like butter.

I like jam.

I like eating

purple ham!

Here, is, a, for, my, little

Here is a glass.

Here is a cup.

Here is a bowl

for my little pup.

come, to, me, said, you

"Come to me,"

said Mr Tree.

"I'll come to you,"

said Mrs Shoe.

We, are, up, in, the

We are running.

We are skipping.

We are jumping high.

We are hopping.

We are flying

high up in the sky.

in, out, is, with, his, has, a

In, out, in, out,

Pig is digging

with his snout.

Out, in, out, in,

Pig has found

a safety pin.

I, up, down, and, a, like

I jump up

and I jump down.

Up like a pup,

and down like a clown.

look, at, the, with, on

Look at the clown
with the bike.
Look at the clown
with the hat.
Look at the clown
on the wire,
and look at the clown
on the mat.

Little Lilly Lolly Legs, little, red, blue

Little Lilly Lolly Legs
has lots of little clothes pegs.
Little red and little blue,
Little Lilly Lolly Lou.

I, can, make, a, the

I can make a pie.
I can paint the sky.
I can make a hat.
I can paint the cat.

We, and, the

We ran, and we ran, and
we ran, and we ran.
We ran all over
the frying pan.

go, going, got on

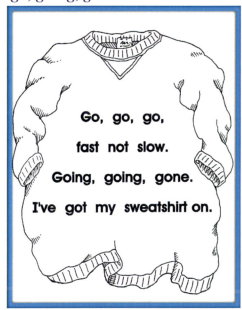

Go, go, go,
fast not slow.
Going, going, gone.
I've got my sweatshirt on.

see, my, big, and, it

See my big toe.
See my big toe.
See it wiggle,
and see it squiggle.

39

- **PLAY** card games such as Snap, Fish and Memory.

> *" Do you have **the**?"*
> *"Do you have **go**?"*

- **USE** plastic letters to demonstrate how to make and break words. Work with a small group of children and start with simple, three-letter words such as *big*.

* Provide a model if necessary.

* Provide only the letters required to make the word.

* Provide a written model if necessary.

* Lay the letters out randomly.

* Have the children make the word.

* If using a model, ask the children to check with the model to make sure they are right.

* Have the children read the word they have made.

* Gradually withdraw the model so that children have to remember the word.

When children have an understanding of making and breaking words, they can play this game in pairs or small groups.

One child chooses the word and selects the letters. The child then rattles the letters like dice, scatters them and tells another the word.

The second child makes the word. The first child checks the word.

There are many ways of teaching word recognition. We have found the most valuable are those that are meaningful to children because they arise from work that they are engaged in rather than isolated skills and drills.

Further suggestions for learning high-frequency words are found in Chapter 4.

Learning new words and imprinting them into long-term memory is essential to learning to read successfully.

Children can increase their vocabulary in a couple of ways: by learning new word meanings (vocabulary) and by recognizing new words in print (word recognition). Introducing children early on to the high-frequency words can help them build a strong foundation for further learning. Once taught, vocabulary and word recognition will build on themselves.

4
Getting Under Way with Writing

> *"How can I help my children get under way with writing?"*
>
> *" I usually let my children choose their own topics, but some just don't get going, and others write the same thing every day. What can I do about this?"*

Six Guidelines for Writing

The following six guidelines can help you get your children off to a good start with writing as soon as possible.

1. **EXPECT** that the children will write. Teacher expectation is a great motivator and has proven results (Good and Brophy, 1981). What teachers expect, providing the expectations are realistic, children will produce.

2. **ENSURE** that the children have a pencil in their hand and are writing messages every single day.

3. **DESIGNATE** time for writing messages that is not handwriting instruction. Also provide time and materials so that children can choose to write independently as a free choice activity.

4. USE authentic contexts to model and demonstrate writing so that children understand not only the different forms of writing but also different purposes and audiences. For beginning writers these may be personal narratives, letters, labels and lists.

5. WORK from what the children can do and help them towards what they are trying to do.

6. KNOW the four main strategies that children need to be able to control to become independent writers and know the degree of control any child has over any strategy at any point in time. The four main early writing strategies are hearing and recording sounds in words; spelling some words correctly every time; making orthographic analogies; and using people and resources to help. Careful observation is required.

Below are examples of different ways that children can be encouraged to use four strategies in a guided writing lesson.

Marcia has been at school for six months. She is very articulate and can quickly produce a sentence from her own experience when it is writing time. She also knows many alphabet letters and sounds and can write some short high-frequency words on her own. When her group has been working with plastic letters, Marcia has shown

that she can make word families by changing the initial letter or onset and leaving the rime (rhyming segment) the same. In this interaction, Marcia is working in an individual situation with her teacher, Paul.

Marcia's sentence is

"I went to the store with my Dad to get a tent for camping."

Paul quickly jots down the sentence on a jotter pad that he carries with him and analyses it in terms of what Marcia can already write.

His analysis looks like this:

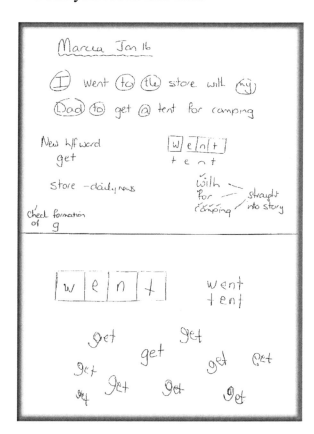

The words circles are those words that he knows that Marcia can write. He will expect that Marcia will write these in her story correctly without any help.

44

Paul quickly makes decisions about the next most important learning for Marcia. He decides that she can learn *get* to increase her bank of known words. He will use *went* as the word that Marcia will hear and record using the Elkonin boxes and encourage her to write *tent* using an orthographic analogy. Marcia will know where to find the word *store* because it was part of that morning's Daily News. The rest of the words he will work on with Marcia straight into her story.

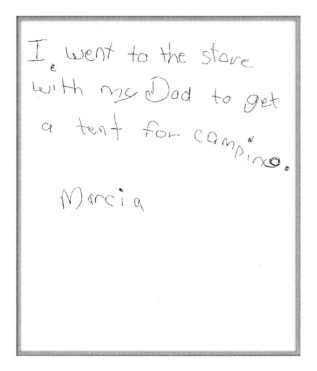

Marcia writes her story on a piece of paper that she will illustrate later. Paul uses his jotter pad to work with Marcia on her story. At the end of the session he will tear off this paper and put it in Marcia's file. In this way he has a record of progress.

Paul now has a complete record of Marcia's progress in learning new short high-frequency words, hearing and recording sounds, making analogies and using the environment.

In another situation, Paul is working with a group of four children during guided writing. Each child is writing an individual message based on the part they like best from a shared story. Three of these children have been at school less than three months.

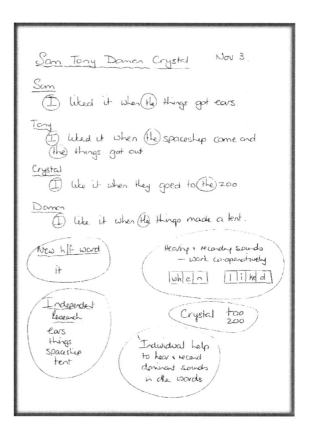

The children's sentences that Paul has jotted down are

Sam *I liked it when the things got ears.*

Tony *I liked the part when the spaceship came and the things got out.*

Crystal *I like it when they goed to the zoo.*

Damon *I like it when the things made a tent.*

45

His teaching decisions are as follows.

Everyone can write *I, the* and *a.* A good new word to learn would be *it* because it is nice and short and it appears in everyone's sentence. Paul decides that everyone can hear and record the sounds in *like(d)* and *when* co-operatively as those words appear in each child's sentence. The children have access to the book to either search for or check on their approximated spelling of *ears, things, spaceship, zoo* and *tent.* He will work individually with the children helping them hear and record as many other dominant sounds as they can, and/or he will talk to them about their approximated spelling attempts. He will work with Crystal only on making analogies because the other children have not yet shown that they can use this strategy with plastic letters. With Crystal he will use the word *too*, which she knows, to help her write *zoo*.

Paul has found that when he works like this with a small group of children, they tend to help and learn from each other as well as learning from him.

Strategies for Early Writing

Hearing and Recording Sounds in Words

Children need to be able to make the connection between the sound of oral language and the symbol that represents that sound in print. You will know when a child has made such a connection because he or she may write *L* for *elevator* or *WDO* for *window*.

Many children may arrive at school already having made this connection. They need to progress from these beginnings to the ability to hear and record sounds in words in sequence.

Spelling Some Words Correctly Every Time

All children need to have a bank of known words that they can spell correctly every time. This applies particularly to their names and the short high-frequency and high-interest words that they use regularly in their writing. The children will be much more efficient at writing when they have words that are secure, habituated, and fluent, rather than having to sound them out each time they wish to write them. Second, many short high-frequency words do not lend themselves to sounding out for correct spelling. For example, those letters with silent *e* endings such as *like, have* and *here*; those letters that start with *wh*, such as *when, where, what*; and those with unusual spelling or pronunciation patterns, such as *who* and *are*.

Making Orthographic Analogies

Children need to know how to make orthographic analogies, that is **use known spelling patterns to spell new words.** Although it is often said that English spelling is irregular, there are, in fact, many regularities among irregular spellings. For example, *ight*, is called an irregular spelling pattern, yet its pronunciation is constant in the many words that end with *ight*.

For example, *blight, bright, fight, flight, fright, light, might, night, plight, right, sight, slight, tight.*

Research into orthographic analogies and onset and rimes shows that very young children can make links between known and new words when the word call the onset and the rime (Goswami, 1988, 1994; Goswami and Mead, 1992).

The **onset** is the initial consonant or consonant cluster.

The **rime**, often a rhyme, is the vowel and any consonants that follow it.

For example, in the word *cat, c* is the onset, and *at* is the rime; in the word *string, str* is the onset, and *ing* is the rime. For a more detailed explanation see page 9 in Chapter 1.

From the following thirty-five dependable rimes, children can make nearly five hundred words. The rime is called **dependable** because in each case the rime has the same rhyme. For example, all the words that end with *ame,* such as *came*, rhyme with *came*. All the words that end with *ight*, like *night,* rhyme. There are many other rimes that are not dependable, although many of the endings may rhyme. For example, *and* rhymes with *band, hand, land, sand* but does not rhyme with *wand.*

Thirty-Five Dependable Rimes

ack   ail   ain   ake   ale   ame   an   ank   ap   ate   aw   ay

eat   ell   est

ice   ick   ide   ight   ill   in   ine   ing   ink   ip   it

ock   oke   op   ore   ot

uck   ug   ump   unk

Using People and Resources to Help

There will be times when children will not be able to use any of the first three mentioned strategies to assist with their writing and other times when these strategies will not be as effective as using a person or a print or electronic resource. For these reasons, children also need to know how and where to look for assistance for words they wish to write or words they wish to check while editing their work.

Children need to know where to look for interesting words that have occurred recently in topic studies, news stories or books. For example, a child writing a report about dinosaurs may refer to a big book that has been part of the thematic study to spell *brontosaurus*.

What is important is that the children have a range of strategies to call upon rather than just relying on sounding out. Your job is to help them learn how and when to use each of these

Teaching Children How to Hear and Record Sounds

• **DEMONSTRATE** how to hear and record sounds by thinking aloud during shared writing. For example, during the Daily News, your thinking aloud may sound like this:

*"The first word I need is **today**. Now how
will I start it? /t,/ /t/, /t/, that's right – it starts the same as **television**. I know that one is capital **T**."*

Encourage the children to participate as much as possible by asking them to hear the dominant consonants, especially the initial and final ones in the words you want to write. When they can hear the sound, ask which letter they would expect to see. Make the links for them using your class alphabet frieze or alphabet chart if necessary, so that they

• **USE** the Daily News to elicit from the children words that start with the focus letter in the story. For example, if the focus letter was *m*, you might create the Daily News like the example (shown right) and include other words that start with *m* that the children in the class can supply.

The Daily News is a good way to explore focus letters and initial sounds.

• **PLAY** word games.

"I'm thinking of a word that starts like **monkey***. It's something you use to buy things.*
It's called _____."

• **PLAY** games such as I Spy.
"I spy with my little eye something beginning with s."

Daily News

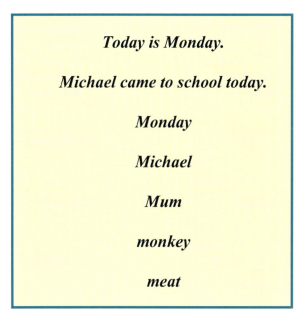

Today is Monday.

Michael came to school today.

Monday

Michael

Mum

monkey

meat

• **USE** magazine research to find pictures that begin with the same sound. Use them to make a chart.

• **MATCH** the letters to the pictures.

• **USE** jingles to reinforce sounds. Children can hear the sounds and see the letters. You may want to use the same poems and jingles that you used for learning alphabet letters.

• **WORK** with a small group of children during writing time. Teach them how to hear and record the sounds as they are writing their messages. Help them link the sound to the symbol. Use individual alphabet cards for each child to keep in their books or your alphabet frieze or chart if necessary.

You may say,

> *"Maria's story is,*
> **'I like red flowers.'**
> *Maria has written **I**."*

Ask her to say the next word slowly and listen for the sounds she can hear. Say it with her if she is unable to do it by herself. Emphasize the dominant sounds for her until she can hear them. When she can hear a sound, ask her what letter she will write. If she cannot write it, provide a model for her to copy. If she can isolate the sound, but does not know the letter symbol, use the alphabet chart to help her make the link,

> *l   leaf*
> *   like*

Let her write the *l* in herself. Repeat the procedure with *i* and *k* . Write the silent *e* for her. Continue with **red** and **flowers** in the same way.

50

The conversations between you and Maria for the word *flowers* may go something like this:

Teacher: What is the next word in your sentence?
Maria: *flowers.*
Teacher: Say it slowly, listen for the sounds, and see if you can work out how to start writing *flowers.*
Maria: /f/l/ow/ers/.
Teacher: Say it again slowly. What can you hear first?
Maria: /f/.
Teacher: Good listening, do you remember which letter you need?
Maria: f
Teacher: OK. Write it down and now say *flowers* again. Let's see if we can hear the next sound. (*Demonstrates emphasizing and stretching out the /l/. /f/lllllll/ow/ers/.*)

Maria: /l/.
Teacher: Excellent, remember it looks like the one that starts *leaf* and you just wrote it in your story to start the word *like*. (*Maria writes l. The teacher writes ower.*)
Teacher: Now we've got *flower*. What shall we put on the end to make it into *flowers?*
Maria: s. (Writes *s*.)

• **SPEND** fifteen minutes with each group while the others write independently or engage in independent writing related tasks. It is not necessary for you to finish each story with each child. Your purpose is to teach them how to hear and record sounds when they are writing.

The purpose of lessons, such as teaching children to hear and record sounds, is to give children a tool to assist them with independent writing. It is possible to work with a small group of four children this way as you would for guided reading. Often the children will be able to help each other with the sound-symbol connections.

Using the Elkonin Boxes

For children who are experiencing great difficulty matching sound to symbol, you may need to draw a box for every sound in the word they are trying to write. Have the child push markers into the box as they say the sound. This technique is derived from the Russian psychologist Elkonin and is known as the Elkonin Boxes (Elkonin, 1973).

The process for using the Elkonin Boxes is as follows.

Learning the Task

Your goal is for children to be able to perform this task independently. To ensure that this will happen, it is imperative that you take time at the beginning to teach them the task. This will include teaching children how to articulate a word slowly, how to listen for the sounds as they articulate the word, and how to push markers as they articulate the word.

- **USE** familiar pictures with no more than four easily recognizable sounds to teach the task. Familiar animals such as a cat, goat and tiger make good examples.

- **MOUNT** the pictures on separate cards and draw boxes for each sound below the picture. Make sure to leave enough space at the bottom of the card below the boxes for the markers.

- **DEMONSTRATE** how to say the word slowly, stretching it out. Do not break the word into phonemes as you articulate it.

- **ASK** the child to say the word slowly. Children often need practice to do this, and you should have them persevere until they are able to stretch the word out appropriately.

- **DEMONSTRATE** how to stretch out the word and push the markers at the same time.

- **ASK** the child to do this independently but assist if necessary.

Teaching the task should not take more than one or two sessions. Children need not be able to make a perfect match between articulation and moving markers before you move to the next step.

Hearing Sounds and Writing Letters

As soon as the child has mastered the task using pictures and markers, start him or her using the task to help spell words they need to write.

- **CHOOSE** a word from the child's sentence. The word you choose should be regular in spelling, easily segmented into phonemes, and contain some of the sounds that you know the child can match with alphabet letter symbols. Choose words such as *go* and *big* rather than *who* or *because*. If, for example, the child's sentence is,

I went to the store with my Dad to buy a tent for camping.

there are many opportunities for using the Elkonin boxes. You may choose *went, store, my Dad, tent.* You will not want the child to work on all these words as it will be too much new learning and take too much time. To help with your choice, it is advisable to analyse the child's sentence in terms of what he or she can already write, and the other writing strategies that the child has to learn. Refer to page 44 earlier in this chapter for an example of this analysis. Aim to work on only one or two words per lesson using the Elkonin boxes.

• **WORK** on the word when the child is ready to write it in his or her sentence. Do not work on the word before the child starts writing or at the end of the lesson.

• **DRAW** the appropriate number of boxes for the child using a small dry erase board, a piece of paper or part of the child's writing book that is designated for practice. Use a pencil to draw the boxes so that the lines are unobtrusive.

• **ASK** the child to articulate the word and move the markers as you did when teaching him or her the task. Beware of falling into the trap of articulating the word for the child. It is easier for children to hear the sounds when someone else does the articulation, but it does not teach them to become independent.

• **ASK** the child which sounds he or she can hear. If you know the child can write the corresponding alphabet letter, you can ask him or her to do so. If the child can name the letter but is unable to write it, provide a model for the child to copy. If the child can hear the sound but is unable to identify the corresponding alphabet letter, make a link for the child to something he or she knows well. This may be a familiar object or the name of a child in the class. These links are very important for some children as they help them make connections that are otherwise too difficult.

• **ACCEPT** what the child can hear no matter what the order in the very early stages. You will find that most children soon start listening for the initial sound first, but some children find it easier to hear dominant final consonants in the beginning stages.

• **REPEAT** the process by having the child articulate the word again and move the markers until he or she has heard and recorded all the sounds that you know they are capable of. In the very early stages you would expect the child to hear dominant consonants and some dominant vowels.

• **WRITE** in those letters that the child is unable to. Where two graphemes correspond to one phoneme, write both the letters in the same box.

b	*oa*	*t*
m	*a*	*de*

- **ACCEPT** appropriate analysis of words even though it may not correspond to regular spelling patterns. If the child hears and records *k a t* for cat, praise the child for hearing the appropriate sound and point out the mismatch.

Later Learning

As the children become more competent you can make the following changes:

- **ALTER** your questioning. Instead of asking, "What sounds can you hear? Which letter will you write?" ask, "What letter do you expect to see?" This encourages children to start using both the phonemic and graphic cues together rather than separately.

- **DRAW** a box for each letter rather than each sound, so that children start to become aware of conventional spelling patterns.

- **DISPENSE** with the markers and ask the children to use their fingers to signal the box that they are going to write the letter in.

- **ENCOURAGE** the children to write the words directly into their story, and use the boxes only for difficulties.

Learning High-Frequency Words

The following words are those that children use most often in their writing. These words were taken from analysing a ten-minute writing test of one hundred children, age six.

High-Frequency Words

The go he is in I me to a my and look

it no we at be like can see she up big

on so you am by an come do for going

not got here his into some yes as are

came down get have her him little make off

one out today went that this play run jump

Overlearning is the key to knowing how to write these words. Children need to see the words, make the words with plastic letters, and write the words many, many times before they will know them. To encourage their learning, you may consider some of the following activities.

• **HAVE** the children use plastic letters. Make the word, read the word, and break the word. Later, encourage them to make the word, read the word, cover the word, write the word, check the word, read the word. (Children may peek at the word if necessary while they are learning to write it correctly.)

• **USE** dry erase boards or magic slates. Write the word over and over until it is learned, erasing each time. This is a writing task, not a copying task. If the child is using paper and pencil, fold the paper over each time or use another paper or card to cover the previous word. If the child needs a model to start with, provide it. Then cover it and allow the child to peek if necessary. Then remove it altogether. Encourage the children to make sure the words are

• **ENCOURAGE** the children to spell the high-frequency words for you to write in the Daily News story or your specific writing demonstration. Have some children come and write the high-frequency words directly into the news story for you.

• **PROVIDE** a list of high-frequency words in the back of each child's writing journal for reference. Each time the child writes the word correctly, the more habituated it becomes.

High-Interest Words

The most common high-interest word was the child's first name followed by

cat   dog   Mum   red   Dad   car   bed   love   zoo   blue

yellow   black   and   the child's surname

• **PROVIDE** simple spelling cards for the children to use. Ensure that in the early stages words that look alike are not on the same card. Number the back or colour code the cards in order of difficulty.

You may want to demonstrate to the class how to use the cards and then place them in the reading centre for students to use independently.

1	2	3	4	5
he	is	in	at	for
I	and	am	of	on
to	my	we	that	it
a	he	here	was	went
				up

6	7	8	9	4
going	have	this	look	his
are	me	with	get	so
like	can	had	as	they
said	not	but	be	got
you	go	all	him	come
			one	big

11	12	13	14	15
she	little	make	about	were
will	made	new	been	an
too	now	some	came	before
from	only	the	down	could
if	see	when	which	her
did	there	because	who	where

Using the Spelling Cards

- Introduce the first card to the children.
- Tell the children the words on the card.
- Explain the steps for learning the words.

Steps for Learning the Words

- Say the word.
  Ask someone if you don't know it.

- Look at the word.

- Say the word.

- Trace the word with your finger, saying the word as you trace it.

- Copy the word, read it, copy it again, read it.

- Place your hand over the word and see if you can write it. Peek if you need to.

- Check the word you have written.

- Read what you have written.

- Keep writing the word without copying until you know it.

- Say the word each time you write it.

- Take a picture of the word with your invisible camera and put it in your head.

- Shut your eyes and see if you can see it.

- Write it again.

- When you think you know all the words on the card ask a friend to check you. Your friend says the word, and you write it. Your friend will let you peek if you need to.

- When you can write all the words on the card without peeking, come and show the teacher how clever you are.

- After the teacher has checked, he or she will give you the next card.

- **NOTE** on a master list which words each child has mastered. Expect to see evidence of this correct spelling in the children's writing. If you do not, insist that the children correct these misspellings for themselves.

- **PROVIDE** a guided reading creative response that requires the children to write the word in a meaningful context. Give the children a sentence starter to copy and complete. For example:

*I like the part when*_____.

*My best character was*_____.

Make sure the children copy the sentence starter because in this way they are practising the high-frequency word.

Using Orthographic Analogies

It is sometimes more efficient for children to use larger chunks of information that they know than to try to sound out individual phonemes.

For example, to write the word *sand,* the child may sound out /s/a/n/d/ or may recognize that the word rhymes with *and*, which is a known word. Using known words is quicker and often more reliable. However, before children can use onsets and rimes to assist with reading or writing, they need to be able to hear rhymes.

Ways to Help Children Learn Rhymes

- **USE** simple jingles, poems and nursery rhymes to help children to hear the rhymes.

- **USE** oral cloze procedures, such as, *Hickory Dickory Dock, The mouse ran up the* _____.

Introduce these jingles to the children and have them stick them into their individual jingle books. The children can then hear and see the rhymes as they read them.

The following jingles contain some of the frequently used rimes that children will need.

-ide, -ump

Maisie Maisie Muddledy Mide,

Let me take you for a ride.

First we will jump

over the hump.

Then we'll ride back

with a bumpety bump.

-ack

Mary Mack

had a dress that was black,

with a big, red bow

in the middle of the back.

She carried her lunch

in a purple pack,

and her high-heeled shoes

went clickety clack.

-ump, -ip

Jump and thump,

jump and thump,

all the way

to the rubbish dump.

Trip and skip,

trip and skip,

all the way

to the pirate ship.

Meat and cake,

meat and cake.

I like eating

meat and cake.

Meat and cake,

meat and cake.

What a lot

of mess you make.

Freddy Fusspot got a fright

when he opened

his bathroom door last night.

In his bath

were some yellow mice

playing with a spotted dice.

Vegetables, vegetables in the pot.

What a lot of soup you've got.

Drink and eat, drink and eat,

drinking soup is really neat.

Sit on a mat,

and knit a hat.

No, no, no,

I can't do that.

Ring the bell,

ring the bell.

I can't do that,

I don't feel well.

The king

with the ring

played with some string.

The skunk,

who had shrunk,

played with some junk.

- **PLAY** word games.

"I'm thinking of a word that rhymns with flag. I bring it to school every day. It's called my _____?"

- **USE** plastic letters.

Always work with a word that the children know so that they are building new knowledge on known knowledge, not going from unknown to unknown.

The following example uses the word *cat*.

* Give each child a the plastic letters *c a t s h.*

* Make the word *cat* with plastic letters and ask the children to make *cat* with their plastic letters.

* Ask the children to check their response against your model to ensure they are correct. If they are unsure, ask them to jumble the letters and make *cat* again.

* Move the *c* away from *at* explaining what you are doing and what you have left.
*"Look, if I take the **c** away from **cat** I am left with **at.**"*

* Ask the children to do the same with their letters.

* Put *s* in front of *at* and draw the children's attention to what you are doing by running your finger underneath and saying,

*"Look, if I put an **s** in front of **at**, it makes **sat.**"*

* Ask children to do the same with their plastic letters.

* Repeat the procedure with *h* to make *hat* and *b* to make *bat.*

* Verbalize what you are doing each time and ask the children to do the same.

* Make *cat, bat, sat* or *hat*, and ask the children to read the words.

* Repeat this with different words until the children are confident in their responses.

* Invite the children to make a word and ask you or a partner what they have made.

* As the children become more confident with rime analogies, you could introduce an initial letter cluster, such as *flat.*

• **FOLLOW** the same procedure using dry erase boards and markers or pencil and paper.

• **MATCH** rhyming pictures, such as,
    cat, hat
    dog, frog.

• **MAKE** a rhyme montage from magazine pictures or drawings.

• **MAKE** rhyme spirals or mobiles.

It is not important for the children to know all the words that they are making. What is important is that they know how to go from a known word to make or solve (that is write or read) an unknown word.

Helping Children Compose Messages

There are two common problems that some young children can face when asked to write every day. The first is generating a message; the second is generating a different message each day.

Some children find exceedingly difficult to generate a message because they do not control the appropriate English language structures, or they do not have experiences that they wish to call on, or they are unwilling to take risks, feeling that their current level of expertise precludes them from writing. For similar reasons some children perpetuate the same story every day: *"I went to the park."*

For these children it is important that you provide a balance in the writing programme that will allow them to write from personal experience and will also introduce them to other forms of writing.

Exploring Shared Experiences

Shared experiences as motivation for writing are extremely important for beginning writers. As well as providing a basis for writing, they also help children explore, understand and talk about the world around them. They provide opportunities for close observation, which is the mark of all excellent writers. Shared experiences can also encourage problem solving, provide for the arrangement of ideas, and the drawing of conclusions. Shared experiences also provide the link between oral and written language, as children are first engaged in talking about what they are going to write about. In this instance, the children are able to use their own oral language patterns, and the teacher can extend their knowledge by providing alternative models.

Ideas for Shared Experiences

- **TALK** and write about unplanned experiences such as:
  * The weather – an unexpected thunder-storm, or snowstorm.
  * Visits from parents or guests.
  * Workers in the school.
  * The fire alarm.

- **TALK** and write about planned experiences such as:

  * Descriptions – look at your hand under a magnifying glass.
  * Guessing games
    What is in this bag?
  * Children's shared experiences on the playground or a field trip.
  * Dealing with anger, fear or criticism.
  * Photographs and pictures.

Procedures for Using a Shared Experience for Writing

1. Decide on the shared experience.

2. Share the experience and allow children to talk freely about it.

3. Compose a class story about the experience in a shared writing situation. Have the children dictate the story and encourage them to help you spell the words they know.

4. Read the story together.

5. Have the children write their own responses to the experience. Some children will be able to do this independently; others will need to use the class story as support.

6. Encourage the children to share their own stories with their classmates.

7. Publish and display the children's stories as individual books illustrated by the children or as a large book of short stories with appropriate illustrations.

8. Put the books in an accessible place and use for free reading.

- **TALK** and write about imaginary things:

  * The day the fire-eating dragon came to school.
  * My day with the children from Saturn.
  * When our class went to the middle of the earth.

- **INVESTIGATE,** talk and write about

  * Less-familiar objects, such as a green pepper.
  * A new skill
    How I learned to skip with a rope.
  * Classroom pets.
  * Blowing bubbles.
  * What sinks, what floats.
  * Magnets.
  * Taste buds.
  * Making popcorn.
  * Tie-dying, batik, box modelling, or clay.
  * Making music, responding to music.

* **INNOVATE** on existing stories, patterns or themes.

Innovations are valuable sources of writing motivation, and they also encourage thinking about changes that might affect the story – for example, a different ending to a story , a different character, a different description, a different pattern.

Innovations are also valuable because they

* Extend the range of material that children can read independently.
* Enrich ideas and vocabulary.
* Assist with the extension and consolidation of language structures.
* Reinforce the use of high-frequency words.

Any material is suitable for innovations but consider

* Renaming characters.
* Adding episodes.
* Changing endings.
* Writing your own version of the same story.
* Writing a new story using the same structure.
* Writing a whole new story.

If you are using innovations with very young children you may need to isolate just one sentence from the book for innovation, such as

Monster, Monster, big and hairy, how does your growling go?

Procedures for Innovations

1. Read the story that you are going to use for an innovation. A big book is usually suitable for very young children.

2. Isolate the part that you are going to change.

3. Decide which words you are going to change – don't be tempted to

undertake too much with beginning readers and writers.

For example, you may use

Monster, Monster, big and hairy.

Decide whether you will change the noun, *Monster*, or the adjectives *big* and *hairy*. This will result in different innovations. If you change *Monster*, the children will need to think of other things that are big and hairy:

Giant, Giant, big and hairy.
Chimpanzee, Chimpanzee, big and hairy.

If you change *big* and *hairy,* children will have to think of other words to describe the monster:

Monster, Monster, fat and ugly.
Monster, Monster, old and wrinkly.

4. Write the sentence on a chart.

5. Invite children to supply new words.

6. Record the new words above or below.

7. Read the new innovations. Be flexible with this. For many innovations you can mix and match, for example:

Monster, Monster, big and ugly.

8. Invite children to write and illustrate their own innovations. Some children will write completely new innovation; others will still require the support of the class model.

9. Have the children share their innovations.

10. Publish and display the innovations so that they can be used by children during free reading time. If you prefer, instead of writing the innovations on a chart, you can use a felt board and write each word on a card with Velcro on the back. The children can then manipulate these cards to make new stories during free reading time.

- **WRITE** about a story you have just read independently This is particularly appropriate for beginning writers because it

  * Reinforces reading vocabulary.

  * Extends reading and writing vocabulary.

  * Gives the opportunity to write reading vocabulary, search and read again.

  * Provides a model for appropriate English structure, which is reinforcing for some children and new learning for others.

  * Enhances the development of self-concept: *"I've just read that, now I can write about it, too."*

  * Is a productive way for a child to formulate a story as the child has the story in his or her head.

  * Provides for the reciprocal nature of reading and writing – reading being the analysis and writing being the synthesis.

- **USE** sentence starters to write about stories that have been read-alouds, guided, or independent reading.

- **INVITE** the children to retell stories in their own words.

- **HAVE** the children write from a model following a demonstration, such as a short poem.

- **ENCOURAGE** the children to write from a literary model, such as a simple information report or procedure.

- **HAVE** the children write for different purposes, such as signing in at school, or thank-you letters to parents for birthday and Christmas presents.

- **HAVE** the children make lists, such as *"Things I have to do today."*

While children write they learn important strategies that are also appropriate to beginning reading:

* Directionality.
* One-to-one matching.
* Print contains the message.
* Letters are ordered in words.
* Words are ordered into sentences.
* To make predictions.
* To search available knowledge to help form new knowledge.
* To locate and use what they know.
* To check to make sure that they are right.
* To take responsibility for fixing errors where possible.

Beginning writers need to have solid strategies and ample time to practice in order to be successful in their attempts. By following the six guidelines at the beginning of this chapter, you can ensure that your students are consistently getting the time they need to practice every day. By providing them with the four strategies for writing, you can give them the framework they need to use their writing time effectively.

5
Choosing and Using Little Books

"I want to introduce my children to little books that they can read for themselves but they don't know all the words.
How can I help them read these little books?"

"Should I read the books to them first or should I teach them the words first?"

How will I go about choosing the right book?"

The question of when and how to start children reading little books is the subject of much debate. Some teachers feel that children should start with their first little reading books as soon as they start school, while others believe that a firm foundation using shared reading and language experiences is all that is needed during the first year at school. Still other teachers engage in many "reading readiness" activities that have little to do with books, while other teachers believe that early reading can be taught through early writing.

Grouping Children for Instructional Reading

In order to get your children off to a good start as soon as possible, put aside any preconceived beliefs about time spent at school or the best methodologies. The best way to gauge which children can be started on a guided reading programme that uses little books for instruction is to observe carefully what the children are doing.

Find out which children

- Listen attentively while you read to them.

- Participate spontaneously in shared reading and language experiences.

- Choose to "read" books during free choice time.

- Know how to handle books.

- Understand some of the conventions of print, for example, where to start reading, the direction to read the book and that the print, not the picture, tells the story.

- Respond appropriately in language plays, poems and jingles that contain rhyme and alliteration.

- Know some alphabet names and their corresponding sounds.

- Recognize one or two words in different contexts.

- Endeavour to match one spoken word to one printed word.

Children exhibiting these behaviours can be gathered together in small groups of two to four for instruction. This instruction should be in addition to the class or group shared reading, language experiences and writing, which should continue for all children.

Choosing Instructional Reading Material for Beginning Readers

When choosing little books for children to read, consider what knowledge they already have that can help them read the book independently.

You need to think about

* What the children already know about the subject matter in the book.

* How many of the language structures in the book the children can control.

* How many of the words the children can already recognize.

* How many letter/letter cluster sounds the children know that will help them predict and check on unknown words.

- How well children can interpret pictures to assist them with their predicting and checking.

- What level of control children have over one-to-one matching of the spoken and printed word.

Taking all these into consideration, you should then choose a book that does not have too much new learning. The importance of prior knowledge cannot be overemphasized. The more information children bring to the reading task, the more they are able to comprehend the author's message. This does not mean that you should either read the book to the children first or preteach the words. If you do this, you will deprive yourself of the opportunity to see which reading behaviours the children control independently. If you choose and introduce the book appropriately, the children will be able to solve the reading problems that they expect to find.

Introducing and Reading the First Little Books

If you want children to be able to read little books independently, while you monitor how well they control strategies, try the following suggestions:

1. **CHOOSE** the book carefully, based on your observations of the children's current knowledge. This may be a book that has only one word per page or it may be a book that has a sentence per page. You will need one book for each child, but do not pass them out at this stage.

2. **TALK** with the children in very general terms about the concepts contained in the book. For instance, of you were using *Mother Hippopotamus*, you would talk about hippopotamuses with the children. You could discuss size, colour, what hippopotamuses eat, where they live, what they do during the day and so on. Wherever possible bring the concepts into the children's personal frame of reference. To do this you may question,

"Who has seen a hippo?
Where did you see it?
What did you think of it?
How did you feel?"

This motivation, or discussion prior to reading , is particularly important because it allows you to find out what the children already know. It is during this discussion that you can extend the understanding of some children, provide consolidation for others, and sort out misconceptions if necessary.

3. INTRODUCE the book to the children by showing them your copy and giving them a synopsis of the plot in one or two sentences. This allows children to link the previous discussion with this particular book. It cues them into which part of the discussion about hippopotamuses is relevant to understanding the author's message.

4. DISCUSS the following book conventions---front cover, back cover, spine, author, illustrator, title page. The children should be familiar with these from their experiences with shared reading, but this is an opportunity for them to demonstrate their understanding on their individual books.

5. DISCUSS the pictures in the entire book with the children. You should discourage them from trying to read at this stage. You are still helping them gain more prior knowledge, which will assist them with the reading task. You are also running past their ears some of the vocabulary and language structures that they will encounter.

There are three important points to remember when discussing pictures.

Don't question the children unless you are sure they know the answer. A wrong response at this stage usually leads to a wrong response during reading. This applies especially to children who do not have labels for the items in the pictures, such as those who may call a tiger a lion, or where there are two labels for the same object, such as couch and sofa.

Children who are just beginning to read usually will not have the letter sound or word knowledge to correct a wrong prediction.

- Don't fall into the trap of reading the text to the children. You want them to have the opportunity to work on new material.

- Keep your discussion of the pictures in the same tense as the book. If the book is written in the present tense, keep the discussion in the present tense. If the book is written in the past tense, use the past tense in your discussion.

6. **GIVE** each child a copy of the book.

7. **TELL** the children they are going to read the whole book all by themselves. Read the title together and ask the children to open their books to the first page and put their finger where they are going to start reading.

8. **REMIND** the children of the strategies that they will need to use to read the book. For the first little books these will be one-to-one matching, directionality and using the picture to help you read the story.

Your instructions may be as follows.

"Turn to the first page and put your finger on the word that you are going to read first in this book. Now remember, every time you say a word, you have to point to a word in the book. Which way are we going to go? And when you finish this page,

where will you go next? If you get stuck, this is what you can do. Go back to the beginning of the page, think about the story in your head, look at the picture to help you, look at the words as you point, and have another try. Now let's start reading the book."

9. **OBSERVE** closely to see which behaviours the children control as they read. Help where necessary with one-to-one matching or with a forgotten word or phrase. It may often be necessary to cue the children into the first page to give them the language structure if the book follows a particular pattern, such as *This is a cat. This is a dog.*

10. **MOVE** around the children and listen to each one read at least one page of the book to you as you go. Note which children need more help and which are confident.

Although you have asked the children to read the whole book themselves and you would therefore expect them to read at different rates, children just beginning often read all together and wait for each other to turn the pages. Less fluent children often listen for the child next to them and then copy.

11. **PRAISE** the children for appropriate reading behaviour.

"Weren't you smart to read that book all by yourselves?"
"I noticed how well you were pointing when you were reading."

12. **CHECK** and deepen comprehension with further discussion.

13. **ASK** children to locate a high-frequency word that occurs regularly in the book. For example, *"Turn to the first page. Show me **in**. Turn over. Show me **in** on this page."And so on.*

17. **CHOOSE** the next most appropriate reading book for the group to read tomorrow, based on the reading behaviours you have observed today. This may be another caption book, another one-line text, a book with two lines of text, another book containing some of the same vocabulary, a book with similar language structures, a book at the same level of difficulty or a book that is harder. Gradually increase the difficulty level while always supporting the children through the introduction and picture discussion.

14. **FOLLOW** the reading with an activity that will revise, consolidate or extend the understanding of the concepts and/or the reading process gained through reading the book. Ideally, this should be a reading, writing or artistic response.

15. **SEND** this little book home for further reading that night, or ensure that the child reads it again to another class member, a buddy from another class or another staff member.

16. **KEEP** one copy of the book in the group "pick and mix" box, a collection of a variety of texts, for further independent reading.

The strategy laid out for introducing your students to little books has been successful in many classrooms in many countries. As they begin to read independently, your students are also learning important lessons about reading: how to hold the book, which way the text flows, word-to-text correspondence and more. By assessing your students as they work at their reading, you will be able to identify which reading strategies they handle confidently and which strategies they need to work on to become truly successful.

6
Putting It All Together

"Now I have all these ideas about what to do, how do I teach them?"

"Is there a set order?"
"Where do I start?"

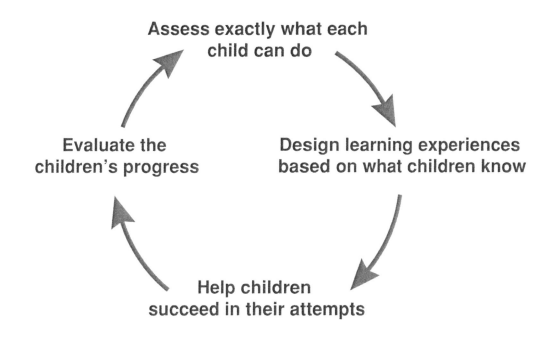

Although putting all these teaching strategies together might seem the hardest step in the process, it is, in fact, the easiest if you put away any preconceived ideas and follow this teaching-learning cycle. This four-step cycle is continuous, and following it allows you to help children to quickly become independent readers and writers.

Assess Exactly What Each Child Can Do

Assessing a child's abilities is best done in the first four weeks of school. You may use a variety of formal and informal observation techniques.

WATCH children in a variety of situations and make anecdotal notes. These situations may be when they are

* Talking to their friends.
* Talking to you.
* Responding to formal questions.
* Participating in language experience and shared reading lessons.
* Reading independently.
* Talking about books they have read.
* Writing.
* Involved in self-directed learning activities.
* Sharing Daily News or their written language.

• **COLLECT** and date samples of work each week. Collect a drawing sample, writing sample and handwriting sample.

• **CHECK** on their ability to

* Write their name.
* Copy their name.
* Trace their name.
* Name the letters in their name.
* Hold the book the right way.
* Turn the pages appropriately.
* "Read" the book by telling the story from the pictures.
* Respond to a read-aloud through naming characters and retelling the plot.

• **NOTE** the following:

* The control each child has over spoken English.
* Which children are risk-takers.
* Which children have a well-developed set for literacy, in that they already recognize some words in reading and between letters and sounds.

• **GATHER** this information into a literacy profile for each child.

Design Learning Experiences Based on What the Children Already Know

Learning is much easier if you start from a known reference point rather than if you try to go from unknown to unknown. For instance, if you find that at the end of the first four weeks most of the children in your class know some of the upper-case alphabet letter names, you do not need to spend time reteaching them. Teach the lower-case letter names using the known upper-case letters as reference points. For example you may say,

> *"You know the name of this letter **B**. This is the big or upper-case **B**. Now here is another letter with the same name. It looks like this **b**. This is the little or lower-case **b**."*

Help the children notice these letters and make links.

• When you are calling the class roll.

> *"Brady begins with **B**."*

• During shared reading.

> *"Here is a word that starts with that little **b**."*

> *"Who can come and show me another word with **b** in it on this page?"*

• When you are dismissing children for lunch or recess.

*"If your name begins with **B**, go and get your snack now."*

- During co-operative story writing.

  *"What letter will I need to start writing **bring?**"*

- During independent literacy activities.

*"Find all the words you can starting with upper case **B** and lower-case **b**. Match the upper-case and lower-case letters."*

By helping children make links you will find that you need not teach all items of knowledge. You need only teach some explicitly and teach others by means of making links or comparisons.

Help Children Succeed in Their Attempts

There are a variety of powerful ways of helping children into new learning.

- **PROVIDE** think-aloud demonstrations. Many teachers provide models or demonstrations for children to emulate. However, sometimes children are not engaged in following the demonstration because they do not understand why the teacher is doing what he or she is doing. By thinking aloud as you demonstrate, you are helping children understand why and how.

"I want to draw a picture of my cat. I will need to put my paper this way because my cat is longer this way. I think I will use an orange crayon because my cat is orange. What else do I need to think about before I

start drawing my cat? That's right I need to make it big on the page and colour it in very brightly so that people will be able to see it when it's on the wall. Now what does my cat look like?"

- **ENGAGE** in some explicit teaching. Most children need explicit teaching of the skills and strategies that will assist them to become readers and writers. Research into early literacy shows that only very able children are able to learn beyond the programme provided (Clay, 1982). Other children need explicit teaching in a wide variety of early literacy behaviours in order to become competent readers and writers.

- **PROVIDE** contexts and structures that will allow children to engage in problem solving. All little children are active problem solvers as they go about their daily work of learning about the world around them. They expect to meet challenges that they can overcome with the help of more experienced and capable adults and peers.

Your role as their reading and writing teacher is to provide literacy settings that will allow this problem solving to occur.

The suggestions for introducing instructional reading texts in Chapter 5, *"Choosing and Using Little Books,"* is an example of providing such a context or structure.

• **QUESTION** the children to help them learn and to allow you to assess their learning.

"What would you do when you come to a word you don't know how to spell?"

"Could you say it slowly and write down the sounds you hear?"

• **ALLOW** time for independent practice. This helps children's skills and strategies to become secure and habituated. Independent practice may be in the same context as previous learning to gain more fluent responses or in a different context to gain fluency and flexibility.

For example, you may ask the children to reread today's little reader to a friend or a doll in the home corner or read from a selection of their familiar little readers each day.

- **GIVE** specific and positive feedback so that children become aware of what they can do and what is the next most important thing for them to learn to do.

"You must feel really good about the way you read that little book."

"I liked the way you managed to match your finger and your voice."

"If you find that you run out of words to point to when you are reading, you could go back and try again from the beginning of the page."

- **PRAISE.** General praise, such as *"Good girl. Good boy. Well done."* means a great deal to young children who seek teacher approval of their actions. It makes them feel successful, and nothing succeeds like success.

Evaluate Progress

Continue to evaluate children's progress and adjust your teaching accordingly. You should do this in the same way as you assessed children at the beginning of the year, by looking, listening, asking, noting and, as children become more capable, simple testing.

The teaching-learning cycle helps children pull together all aspects of literacy learning. The cycle is based on what children can do, rather than a prescribed sequence of learning. The intention is to provide children with skills and strategies that will allow them to function independently as readers and writers.

Blackline Masters

High-Frequency Words   82

First Words in Writing   83

Spelling Cards   84

Jingles   92

High-Frequency Words

Name: _____

up	come	but
we	into	have
a	like	by
and	big	that
go	blue	going
I	all	make
in	are	yes
the	down	here
to	not	this
you	she	will
for	little	of
red	yellow	they
he	said	had
too	no	then
look	be	was
one	so	his
me	am	went
see	on	at
my	out	are
it	an	with
can	did	by
is	get	came
at	away	

First Words in Writing

Name: _____

Child's first name	can	into
cat	see	some
dog	car	yes
Mum	play	love
red	run	zoo
Dad	jump	blue
the	bed	yellow
go	she	black
he	up	are
is	big	came
in	on	down
I	so	get
me	you	have
to	am	her
a	by	him
my	an	little
and	come	make
look	do	off
it	for	one
no	going	out
we	not	today
at	got	went
be	her	that
like	his	this
		Child's surname

Spelling Card 1	Spelling Card 2
the	is
I	an
to	my
a	he

BLM 3

Spelling Card	Spelling Card
3	**4**
in	at
am	of
we	that
here	was

BLM 4 Permission is given to teachers to reproduce this page for classroom use.

85

Spelling Card	Spelling Card
5	**6**
for	going
on	are
it	like
went	said
up	you

BLM 5 Permission is given to teachers to reproduce this page for classroom use.

Spelling Card	Spelling Card
# 7	# 8
have	this
me	with
can	had
not	but
go	all

Spelling Card

9

look

get

as

be

him

one

Spelling Card

10

his

so

they

got

come

big

Spelling Card	Spelling Card
# 11	# 12
she	little
will	made
too	now
from	only
if	see
did	there

Spelling Card 13	Spelling Card 14
make	about
new	been
some	came
them	down
when	which
because	who

Spelling Card

15

were

an

before

could

her

where

BLM 10 Permission is given to teachers to reproduce this page for classroom use.

91

I jump up

and I jump down.

Up like a pup.

and down like a clown.

I can make a pie.

I can paint the sky.

I can make a hat.

I can paint the cat.

Here is a glass.

Here is a cup.

Here is a bowl

for my little pup.

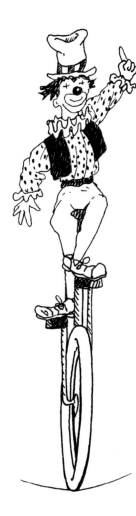

Look at the clown

with the bike.

Look at the clown

with the hat.

Look at the clown

on the wire,

and look at the clown

on the mat.

We ran, and and we ran, and

we ran, and we ran.

We ran all over

the frying pan.

I like butter.

I like jam.

I like eating

purple ham!

BLM 16 Permission is given to teachers to reproduce this page for classroom use.

97

We are running.

We are skipping.

We are jumping high.

We are hopping.

We are flying

high up in the sky.

In, out, in, out,

Pig is digging

with his snout.

Out, in, out, in,

Pig has found

a safety pin.

BLM 18 Permission is given to teachers to reproduce this page for classroom use.

99

Little Lilly Lolly Legs

has lots of little clothes pegs.

Little red and little blue,

Little Lilly Lolly Lou.

Go, go, go,

fast not slow.

Going, going, gone.

I've got my sweatshirt on.

"Come to me,"
said Mr Tree.

"I'll come to you,"
said Mrs. Shoe.

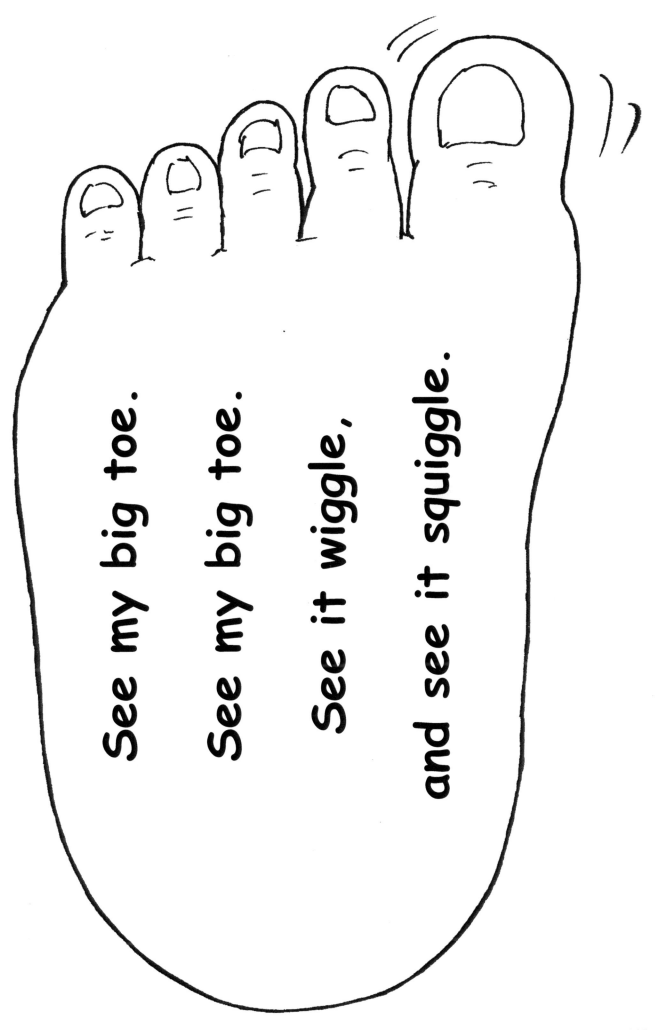

See my big toe.

See my big toe.

See it wiggle,

and see it squiggle.

One yellow bird
flew up in the tree.

One yellow banana
was eaten by me!

Away went the cat.

Away went the dog.

Away went the frog

to sit on his log.

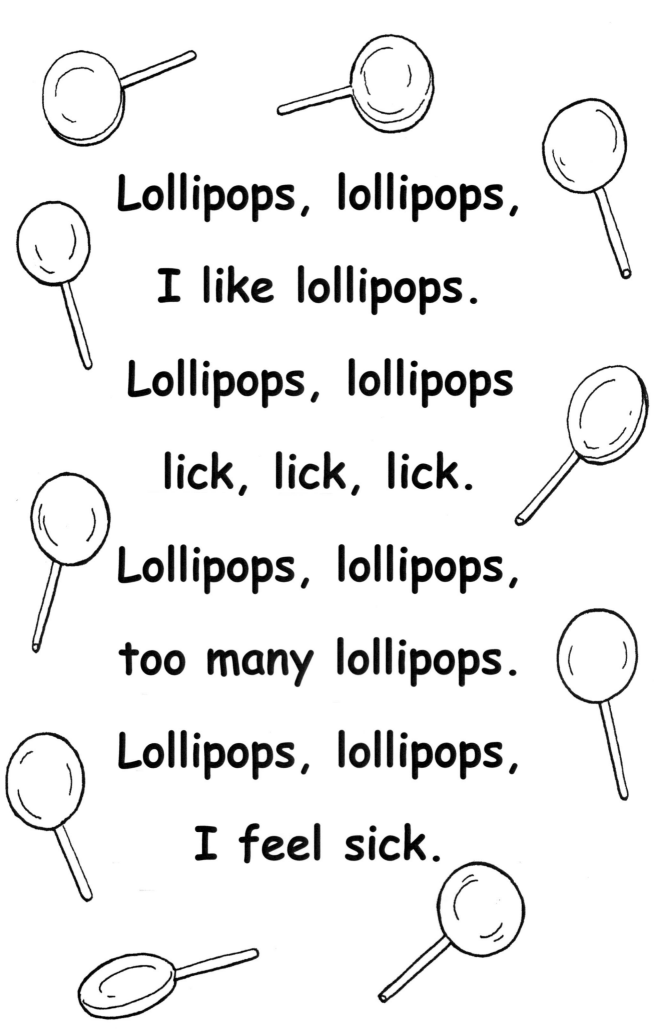

Lollipops, lollipops,

I like lollipops.

Lollipops, lollipops

lick, lick, lick.

Lollipops, lollipops,

too many lollipops.

Lollipops, lollipops,

I feel sick.

Polly Parrot
picks a pear.
Peter Penguin
picks a plum.
Penny picks a pumpkin,
Peter picks a peach,
just one each.

Tippy, tippy, tiptoe
tigers go,
Tippy, tippy, tiptoe
fast and slow.
Tippy, tippy, tiptoe
tigers run.
Tippy, tippy, tiptoe
'round the sun.

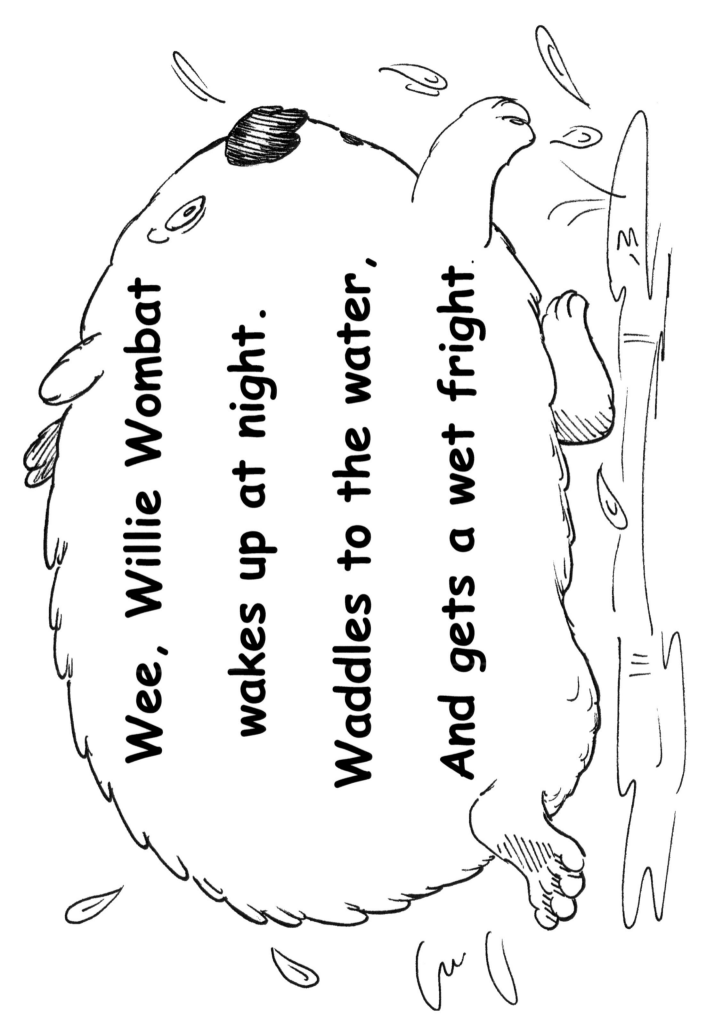

Wee, Willie Wombat

wakes up at night.

Waddles to the water,

And gets a wet fright.

BLM 28 Permission is given to teachers to reproduce this page for classroom use.

109

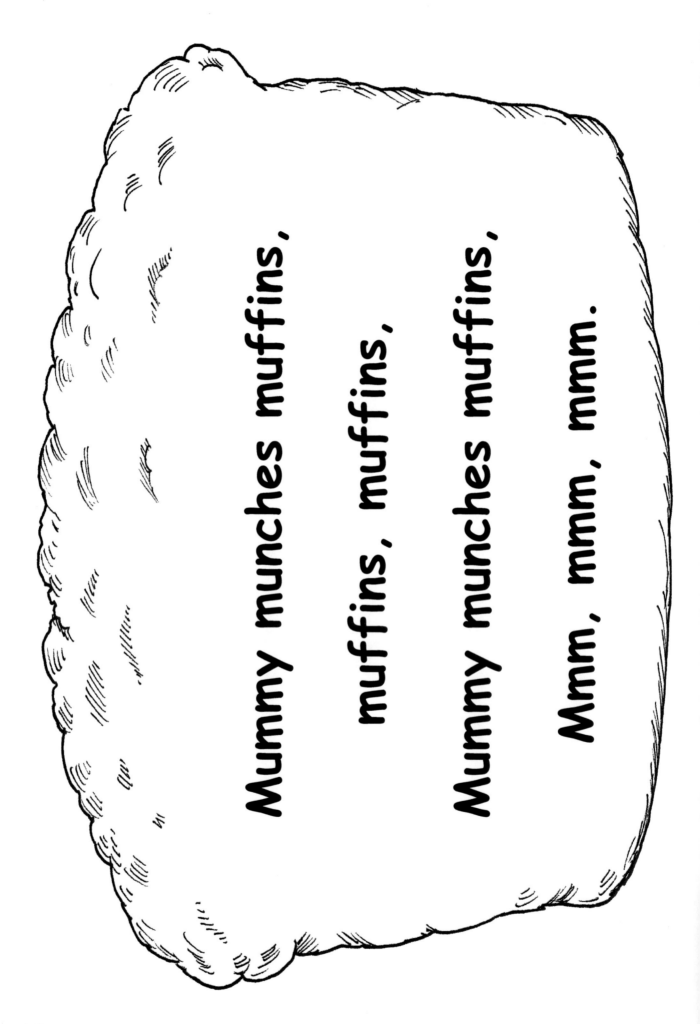

Mummy munches muffins,

muffins, muffins,

Mummy munches muffins,

Mmm, mmm, mmm.

Brian Bertie Baker

blew up a blue balloon.

Brian Bertie Baker ate

biscuits on the moon.

BLM 30 Permission is given to teachers to reproduce this page for classroom use.

111

Harry Hedgehog,

Harry Hedgehog,

hurry, hurry home.

Hang up your hat,

hose the cat,

and feed your garden gnome.

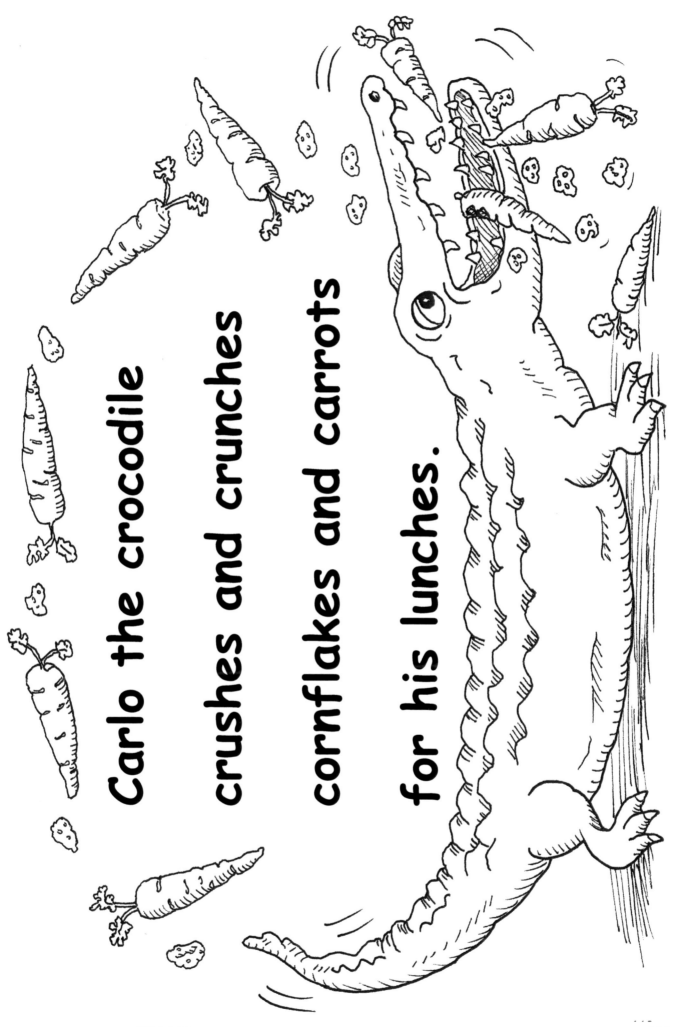

Carlo the crocodile

crushes and crunches

cornflakes and carrots

for his lunches.

Fiddle, fiddle, foodle, fie.

Fishes flying in the sky.

Fiddle, fiddle, foodle, fee.

Fishes frolic in the sea.

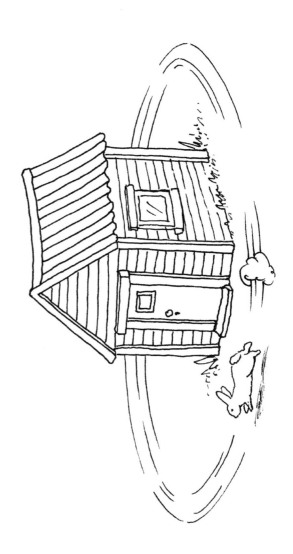

"Run!" roared Rufus Rabbit,

"Run, run, run."

'Round and 'round the red shed,

run, run, run.

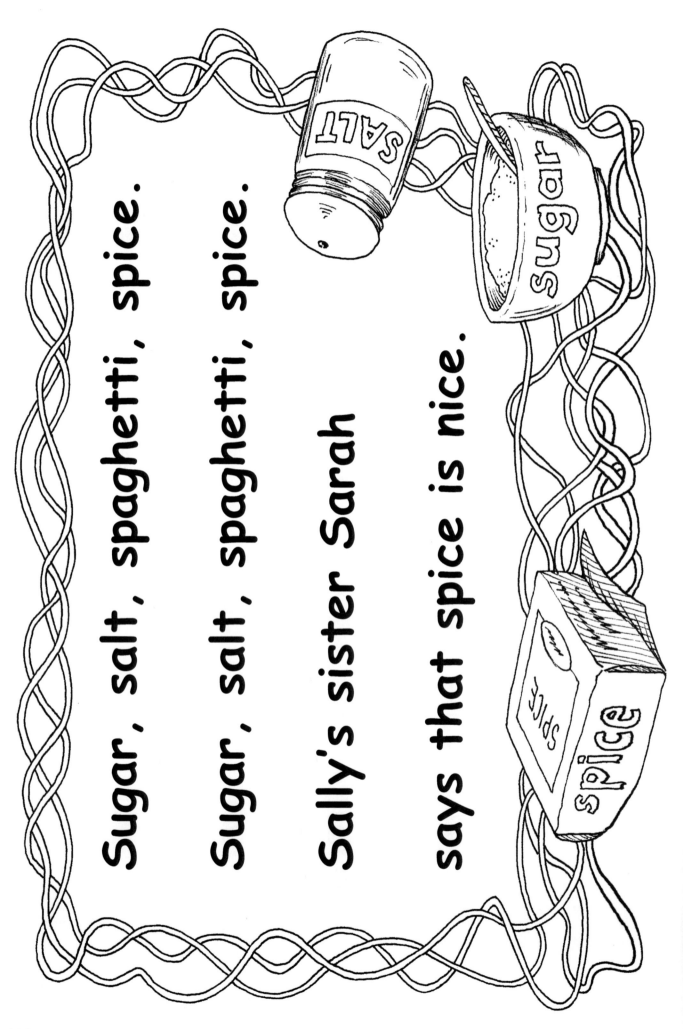

Sugar, salt, spaghetti, spice.

Sugar, salt, spaghetti, spice.

Sally's sister Sarah

says that spice is nice.

Freddy Fusspot got a fright

when he opened

his bathroom door last night.

In his bath

were some yellow mice

playing with a spotted dice.

Maisie Maisie Muddledy Mide,

Let me take you for a ride.

First we will jump

over the hump.

Then we'll ride back

with a bumpety bump.

Mary Mack

had a dress that was black,

with a big, red bow

in the middle of the back.

She carried her lunch

in a purple pack,

and her high-heeled shoes

went clickety clack.

Sit on a mat,

and knit a hat.

No, no, no,

I can't do that.

Ring the bell,

ring the bell.

I can't do that,

I don't feel well.

Jump and thump,

jump and thump,

all the way

to the rubbish dump.

Trip and skip,

trip and skip,

all the way

to the pirate ship.

The king

with the ring

played with some string.

The skunk,

who had shrunk,

played with some junk.

Meat and cake,

meat and cake.

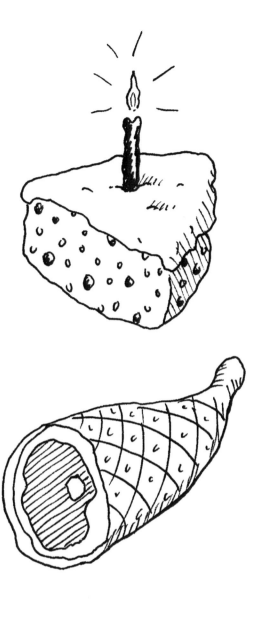

I like eating

meat and cake.

Meat and cake,

meat and cake.

What a lot

of mess you make.

BLM 42 Permission is given to teachers to reproduce this page for classroom use.

123

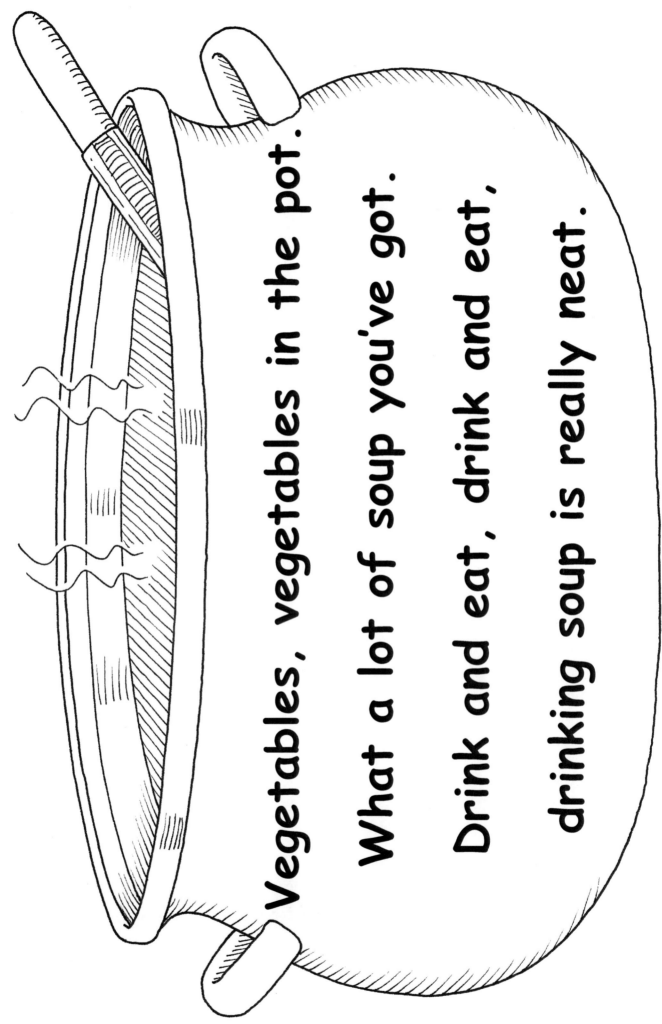

Vegetables, vegetables in the pot.

What a lot of soup you've got.

Drink and eat, drink and eat,

drinking soup is really neat.

References

Clay, M.M. (1982). <u>Observing Young Readers.</u> Exeter N.H. Heinemann.

Elkonin, D.B. (1973). U.S.S.R. In J. Downing (Ed). <u>Comparative Reading</u>, 551-580. New York: MacMillan.

Elley, W.B. (1989). Vocabulary acquisition from listening to stories. <u>Reading Research Quarterly XXIV/2</u>, 314-327.

Good, T.L., & Brohpy, J.E. (1981). Teachers' expectations as self-fulfilling prophesies. In. H.F. Clarizio, R.C. Craid, & W.A. Mehrens (Eds). <u>Contemporary Issues in Educational Psychology, Fourth Edition,</u> 271-277, Boston: Allyn and Bacon.

Goswami, U. (1988). Orthographic analogies and reading development. <u>Quarterly Journal of Experimental Psychology,</u> 40A, 239-268.

Goswami, U. (1994). Reading by analogy: Theoretical and practical perspectives. In C. Hulme, & M. Snowling (Eds). <u>Reading Development and Dyslexia.</u> California: Singular Publishing.

Goswami, U., & Mead, F. (1992). Onset and rime awareness and analogies in reading. <u>Reading Research Quarterly 27</u>, 152-162.

Iversen, S. (1994). <u>The ARP Program.</u> Unpublished Technical Report. Florida: Collier County Department of Education.

Mason, J. M. (1992). Reading stories to preliterate children; A proposed connection to reading. In P.B. Gough, L.C. Ehri, & R. Treiman (Eds). <u>Reading Acquisition.</u> Hillsdale N.J: Lawrence Erlbaum Associates.

Treiman, R.A. (1992). The role of intrasyllabic units in learning to read and spell. In <u>Reading Acquisition.</u> P.B. Gough, L.C. Ehri, & R. Treiman (Eds). Hillsdale N.J: Lawrence Erlbaum Associates.

Wyllie, R.E., & Durrell, D.D. (1970). Teaching vowels through phonograms. <u>Elementary English 47,</u> 787-791.

Index

activities 5, 15-21, 25-30, 55-58, 69, 77, 78

alliteration 70

alphabet 6, 7, 8, 10, 13, 14, 15, 21, 48, 50, 52, 53, 70, 77
  alphabet cards 50
  alphabet charts 48, 50
  alphabet friezes 48, 50
  alphabet letters 6, 7, 8, 10, 13, 14, 15, 44, 50, 52, 53, 77

analogies 9, 11, 45, 46, 47, 58, 62
  orthographic analogies 9, 44, 47, 58
  rime analogies 9, 11, 62

anecdotal notes 77

art work 33

assessment 74, 75, 76, 79, 80

blackline masters 6, 21, 37, 81-124

books 6, 8, 10, 14, 15, 18, 19, 23, 25, 26, 29, 30, 31, 32, 33, 34, 35, 36, 37, 48, 50, 53, 58, 64, 65, 69, 70, 71, 72, 73, 74, 77, 79, 80

big books 18, 25, 29, 31, 33, 36, 37, 48, 65
  book language 8
  book structure 8
  books, conventions of 72
  factual books 25
  little books 35, 69, 70, 71, 72, 74, 79, 80
  picture books 25

charts 19, 24, 31, 33, 48, 49, 50, 65, 66

checking 13, 14, 36, 40, 48, 55, 57, 61, 67, 70, 71, 73, 77

children's published writing 31, 64

class news 34
  (see also *Daily News*)

class stories 62

computers 31

concepts 6, 7, 8, 11, 26, 27, 66, 71, 74
  spatial concepts 27

consonants 9, 14, 47, 48, 53

context 15, 24, 32, 44, 58, 70, 78, 79

cues 8, 11, 54, 72, 73
  graphophonic cues 8,
  semantic cues 8
  syntactic cues 8

curriculum areas 5

Daily News 17, 34, 45, 48, 49, 55, 77

decoding 8, 32

decontextualized language 8

dependable rimes 9, 47, 58

directionality 67, 70, 72

displays 26, 28, 29, 33, 64, 66

Elkonin boxes 45, 52-54

errors, fixing 67

evaluation 75, 80

expectation 30, 43
  teacher expectation 43

explicit teaching 15, 21, 78

finger plays 25

free choice activities 43, 70

free reading 24, 29, 30, 31, 34, 37, 64, 66, 70

games 17, 40, 49, 61, 63

graphemes 13, 53

graphophonic cues 8

guided reading 6, 34, 35, 51, 58, 66, 70

guided writing 18, 44

handwriting 13, 43, 77

heavy-duty letters 13, 14, 20, 21

high-frequency words 14, 34, 35, 37, 41, 44, 46, 54, 55, 58, 65, 73, 82
  short high-frequency words 34, 37, 45, 46

high-interest words 14, 46, 55

independent practice time 15, 19, 79

independent reading 6, 21, 24, 29, 30, 33, 37, 65, 66, 70, 71, 74, 75, 77, 80

independent writing 43, 44, 51, 75, 80

individual little books 35, 69, 70, 71, 72, 74, 79, 80

innovations 29, 34, 64, 65, 66

interest words 14, 46, 55

jingles 25, 37, 50, 58, 70, 92-124
language experiences 13, 27, 29, 34, 69, 70, 77
language patterns 29, 63
language riddles 17
language sounds 8, 10
language structures 8, 65, 70, 72, 73, 74
learning experiences 77
letters 6, 8, 9, 10, 13, 14, 15, 17, 18, 19, 20, 21, 40, 44, 48, 49, 50, 51, 52, 53, 54, 55, 61, 62, 67, 70, 77, 78
  focus letters 17, 49
  heavy-duty letters 13, 14, 20, 21
  letter books 15, 19
  letter cards 18, 20
  letter charts 19
  letter montage 20
  letter names and sounds 6, 13, 15
  letter-sound recognition 7, 8, 13, 46, 48, 50, 52, 53, 77
  letter symbols 50, 52
  letter teaching 13, 14, 15-21
  upper – and lower-case letters 14, 20, 77, 78
listening comprehension 8, 24
listening posts 31
literacy profiles 77
literacy terminology 6, 7-11
literature, stories from 25
little books 35, 69, 70, 71, 72, 74, 79, 80
metacognitive awareness 9
models 6, 29, 30, 40, 44, 50, 53, 55, 61, 63, 65, 66, 67, 78
motivation 6, 43, 63, 64, 71
nursery rhymes 25, 58
observation 44, 63, 70, 71, 73, 74, 76
one-to-one word matching 67, 71, 72, 73
onsets 9, 44, 47, 58
oral cloze 58
oral language 8, 24, 46, 63
  linking oral and written language 63
orthographic analogies 9, 44, 45, 47, 58

phonemes 8, 9, 10, 13, 52, 53, 58
  phonemic awareness 10
  phonemic awareness deficiency 10
  phonemic cues 54
phonics 10, 13, 24
phonological awareness 10
pictures 8, 19, 20, 49, 52, 57, 62, 63, 70, 71, 72, 73, 74, 77, 78
plays 70
poems 18, 20, 25, 31, 32, 33, 37, 50, 58, 70
praise 54, 73, 80
predicting 8, 14, 29, 67, 70, 71, 72
  predicting and checking 14, 70, 71
  predicting text 8
print 6, 23, 29, 32, 41, 46, 48, 67, 70, 71
  conventions of print 70
problem solving 6, 15, 63, 78, 79
progress 5, 45, 46, 80
publishing 31, 64, 66
reading 5, 6, 7, 8, 9, 10, 11, 13, 14, 18, 20, 21, 23, 24, 25, 26, 29, 30, 31, 32, 33, 34, 35, 36, 37, 40, 41, 51, 55, 57, 58, 62, 64, 65, 66, 67, 69, 70, 71, 72, 73, 74, 75, 77, 78, 79, 80
beginning reading 6, 7, 8, 10, 14, 21, 23, 65, 67, 70, 72, 73
free reading 24, 29, 30, 31, 34, 37, 64, 66, 70
guided reading 6, 34, 35, 51, 58, 66, 70
independent reading 6, 21, 24, 29, 30, 33, 37, 65, 66, 70, 71, 74, 75, 77, 80
reading acquisition 7, 9, 10, 11
reading centres 21, 56
reading comprehension 9, 11
reading material 6, 29, 70-71
reading readiness 69
reading strategies 6, 9, 11, 67, 72, 74, 78, 80
reading to children 6, 8, 24, 25, 70, 71, 72

shared reading 29, 34, 36, 37, 69, 70, 72, 77

resources 44, 48

retellings 67, 77

rhyme 9, 10, 25, 37, 44, 47, 58, 61, 62, 70

    rhyme montage 62

    rhyme spirals and mobiles 62

    rhyming pictures 62

riddles 17, 18

rimes 9, 11, 44, 47, 58

    dependable rimes 9, 44, 47, 58

    rime analogies 9, 11, 62

samples 77

self-directed learning activities 77

semantic cues 8

shared experiences 63-64

shared reading 29, 34, 36, 37, 69, 70, 72, 77

shared writing 18, 48, 64

songs 18, 25, 31, 33, 37

sound-symbol relationships 10, 51, 52

spatial concepts 27

spelling 9, 10, 13, 17, 44, 47, 48, 52, 54, 55, 56, 57, 58, 64, 79

    spelling cards 56-57, 84-99

    spelling patterns 54

stories 6, 8, 24, 25, 26, 28, 29, 30, 31,34, 35, 44, 45, 48, 49, 50, 51, 54, 55, 63, 64, 65, 66, 67, 70, 72, 77, 78

class stories 64

strategies 6, 9, 11, 44, 48, 53, 67, 71, 72, 74, 75, 78, 79, 80

    metacognitive strategies 9

    reading strategies 6, 9, 11, 67, 72, 74, 78, 80

    teaching strategies 6, 75

    writing strategies 6, 11, 44, 48, 53 78, 80

subject content areas 5

sustained silent reading 30

syllables 9

syntactic cues 8

teaching strategies 6, 75

topic books 31

traditional tales 25

upper- and lower-case letters 14, 20, 77, 78

vocabulary 6, 8, 9, 23, 24, 25,26, 34, 41, 65, 66, 72, 74

    vocabulary acquisition 8, 23, 24

    vocabulary expansion 6, 9, 24, 25 26, 34, 41

vowels 9, 47, 53

wall friezes 16

wall stories 28, 29, 34

    wall story cycles 28, 29

word games 49, 61

word maps 26

word meanings 6, 23, 24, 41

word recognition 6, 8, 9, 23, 32, 41, 70, 77

word solving 9, 13, 62

word steps 26

words, interest 14, 46, 55

words, learning new 6, 23, 24, 32, 41, 45, 47

words, visual memory of 32

worksheet activities 10

writing 5, 6, 7, 9, 10, 11, 13, 14, 17, 18, 21, 31, 43, 44, 45, 48, 50, 51, 52, 53, 54, 55, 57, 58, 62, 63, 64, 65, 66, 67, 69, 70, 74, 75, 77, 78, 79, 80, 83

    beginning writing 6, 10, 21, 44, 63, 65, 66, 67

    guided writing 18, 44, 45

    independent writing 19, 43, 44, 51 75, 80

    shared writing 18, 48, 64

    writing acquisition 7, 9, 10, 11

    writing journals 55

    writing programmes 63

    writing strategies 6, 11, 44, 48, 53, 78, 80

writing time 43, 50, 67

Level 2
Proof Reading Activiti

Key Stage 2 Age Group 8-10 Years

Make It

R~~ite~~

W~~rite~~

RIGHT!

Photocopiable Masters

Correlated with the Spelling Made Easy
Revised Level 2 Text Book

Spelling Made

Easy

by Ceri Williams

Based on Multi Sensory Structured Phonics Method by Violet Brand

www.spellingmadeeasy.co.uk

Make It Right
Proof Reading Activities
for
Spelling Made Easy Level Two
First published in the United Kingdom in 2015
by Ceri Williams
(based on 'Spelling Made Easy' by Violet Brand)

Copyright assigned to Spelling Made Easy Ltd.
Ceri Williams and Violet Brand (2015)

ISBN 978-1-904421-429

CONTENTS

Make It R~~ite~~ W~~rite~~ RIGHT! ✓
Level Two

Introduction and Biography

		Teaching Points and	Cross References
		page	page
Activity 1.	Short vowel 'a'	2,3	48
Activity 2.	Short vowel 'o'	4,5	48
Activity 3.	Short vowel 'i'	6,7	48
Activity 4.	Short vowel 'e'	8,9	48
Activity 5.	Short vowel 'u'	10,11	49
Activity 6.	'ck'	12,13	49
Activity 7.	'ee'	14,15	49
Activity 8.	'oo'	16,17	49
Activity 9.	'ar'	18,19	50
Activity 10.	'sh'	20,21	50
Activity 11.	'ch'	22,23	50
Activity 12.	'th'	22,23	50
Activity 13.	'or'	24,25	51
Activity 14.	'a' (ā)	24,25	51
Activity 15.	'i-e'	26,27	51
Activity 16.	'o-e'	26,27	51
Activity 17.	'u-e'	28,29	52
Activity 18.	'ai'	28,29	52
Activity 19.	'oa'	30,31	52
Activity 20.	'ir'	30,31	52
Activity 21.	'ou' (ow)	32,33	53
Activity 22.	'ea' (ēā)	32,33	53
Activity 23.	'ur'	34,35	53
Activity 24.	'aw'	34,35	53
Activity 25.	'oi'	36,37	54
Activity 26.	'er'	36,37	54
Activity 27.	'al'	38,39	54
Activity 28.	'ea' (ĕ)	38,39	54
Activity 29.	'ow'	40,41	55
Activity 30.	Silent Letters	40,41	55
Activity 31.	'a' (ar)	42,43	55
Activity 32.	Endings	42,43	55
Activity 33.	'au'	44,45	56
Activity 34.	More Endings	44,45	56
Activity 35.	Letters saying their own name	46,47	56

Make It ~~Rite~~, ~~Write~~, RIGHT!

Introduction

Proof reading is an essential part of written English – it requires visual scrutiny of the passage as well as comprehension, to spot mistakes. These exercises will hopefully develop pupils' reading and spelling skills through guided and individual completion of the activities.

The mistakes written into the text are mainly, but not exclusively, from all the spelling pattern/word families covered in the relevant Spelling Made Easy Teacher's Textbooks and the accompanying 'Fun With Phonics' and 'Spelling Made Easy At Home' series. The aim is further reinforcement and overlearning of the spelling patterns covered in the programme, as well as common High Frequency Words. In the first two levels, aspects of punctuation are confined to capitals at the beginning of a sentence and proper nouns, full stops (periods), and the odd exclamation mark! Punctuation problems increase in complexity throughout the series but are basic in the first two levels, as a flow to the reading is desirable.

Guidelines

- If required, use the first few exercises to model and share the task with the pupil/s. Proof-reading is a skill that requires practice and tuition.

- Read through the passage for meaning and discuss any arising points.

- Get the pupil to follow the words with a 'special' pen/pencil as they or you are reading it.

- Point out punctuation errors and model how sentences sound without full stops especially.

- Re-read and annotate/identify errors. Again, model and share the tasks, especially with reluctant readers and writers.

As the pupils progress through the activities, their particular areas for possible further revision and consolidation work should become apparent through analysis of their answers and responses during lessons.

Ceri Williams

Hey you! Yes you!
Can you help Make It Right?

wrong spellings

There are lots of rong spellins in these bits of

writing.   *spot*

riting. Can you spott them and Make It Right?

some

There are also sume capitals and full stops

missing.   *can*

and speech marks missin See if you kan find

them all!

Good luck!

Ceri Williams

Born in Usk, South Wales, Ceri has taught across primary and secondary phases in both mainstream and special schools. He works in the special needs sector in South Wales. His awards include a Microsoft Innovative Teacher Award, an NGFL-Cymru/Microsoft Innovative Teacher Award and The NAACE Impact Award for Inclusion.

Ceri studied music at The Royal Welsh College of Music & Drama, and education at Birmingham University, initially teaching class music. After relocating back to Wales, he began teaching in the special needs sector, completing a Masters in SEN in 2005 at the University of Newport.

He has presented several papers outlining his work in Multimedia Multisensory Environments at international conferences which have been published in academic journals. As well his interests in education, he still performs frequently as a musician.

Catch The Badger

It was a fakt. Sam and Gus had to acct to cach the jigantic black

and white bajer that lived by the cnal

That bager has tried to snatc Holly's plastick satchl, Gus beegan to say.

You could tell he was angre. "You can see the scrach by the latsh on

the gate were he got in!

Holly said that praps the badger had a famile and that it needed

food and that's wy it tried to dragg the sashel away. Gus hat to

admmit that cud be the case.

"I jest don't wont anyone to get attarcked and hurt, gus sed.

Catch The Badger

fact   act catch gigantic

It was a fakt. Sam and Gus had to acct to cach the jigantic black

   badger   canal.

and white bajer that lived by the cnal

" badger   snatch   plastic satchel," began

That bager has tried to snatc Holly's plastick satchl, Gus beegan to say.

      angry   scratch   latch

You could tell he was angre. "You can see the scrach by the latsh on

   where   "

the gate were he got in!

     perhaps   family

Holly said that praps the badger had a famile and that it needed

     why   drag satchel   had

food and that's wy it tried to dragg the sashel away. Gus hat to

admit could

admmit that cud be the case.

 just want   attacked   " Gus said

"I jest don't wont anyone to get attarcked and hurt, gus sed.

3

The Jogger On The Common

Holly and Harry wer wallking on the comon. They were both very

conteted as they had just ben to a very gud band contets.

Harry promply spoted a joggr as the joger had very brite glosy

running shoes. Harry made a communt as the jogger floped down on

the stop to have a rest from his jogg and tie a not in his shoes again.

"i like the glos on your shoes, they are knokout!" he said.

The jagger wasn'r cros and thanked him for the coplimunt.

"I won't contrudikt you. My bos bought me them as owr company

didn't make a los last year, he said.

The Jogger On The Common

were walking   common

Holly and Harry wer wallking on the comon. They were both very

contented   been   good   contest

conteted as they had just ben to a very gud band contets.

promptly spotted jogger   jogger   bright glossy

Harry promply spoted a joggr as the joger had very brite glosy

comment   flopped

running shoes. Harry made a communt as the jogger floped down on

spot   jog   knot

the stop to have a rest from his jogg and tie a not in his shoes again.

I   gloss   knockout

"i like the glos on your shoes, they are knokout!" he said.

jogger wasn't cross   compliment

The jagger wasn'r cros and thanked him for the coplimunt.

contradict   boss   our

"I won't contrudikt you. My bos bought me them as owr company

loss   "

didn't make a los last year, he said.

Mishap In The Minibus

Holly had been tippd off there was a disko in the distrit youth club

by the brij. She stuk a big distinkt reminder on the frige dor. She

noticed thair was likwid driping down the rij of the frige door and she

wipd it up and had to wrig the cloth out wich hurt her rists a bit.

Later, she and Hary got on the minbus to go to the disc   When thay

got their the club was clozed. Holly loked at the reminder. The date

was a mistak. There was a misprit. The minibus had gon so they had

to get a mimicab home.

Due to the misshap, the driver onle charged the minmum for the

drip home.

Mishap In The Minibus

tipped   disco   district

Holly had been tippd off there was a disko in the distrit youth club

bridge   stuck   distinct   fridge door

by the brij. She stuk a big distinkt reminder on the frige dor. She

there   liquid dripping   ridge   fridge

noticed thair was likwid driping down the rij of the frige door and she

wiped   wring   which   wrists

wipd it up and had to wrig the cloth out wich hurt her rists a bit.

Harry   minibus   disco.   they

Later, she and Hary got on the minbus to go to the disc   When thay

there   closed.   looked

got their the club was clozed. Holly loked at the reminder. The date

mistake   misprint   gone

was a mistak. There was a misprit. The minibus had gon so they had

minicab

to get a mimicab home.

mishap   only   minimum

Due to the misshap, the driver onle charged the minmum for the

trip

drip home.

The Electricity Exam

Harry was revising every sekund for an eggsam in skool. It was all about lectrisity and ellektronix. He ecspectid to do well and, to his credit, had read about sevun tekst-books to ekspand his knowledge.

It was a hecktic spel of wurk and he was feelin a bit on ej. He opend the windo near the egsit, took a deep breaf and took time to ecspel the air unti his lungs was empte. He looked out from the window lej over the hege to the embancmunt.

After all his hard work, he could smel success.

The Electricity Exam

second   exam   school

Harry was revising every sekund for an eggsam in skool. It was all

electricity   electronics   expected

about lectrisity and ellektronix. He ecspectid to do well and, to his

credit   seven text-books   expand

credit, had read about sevun tekst-books to ekspand his knowledge.

hectic spell   work   feeling   edge

It was a hecktic spel of wurk and he was feelin a bit on ej. He

opened   window   exit   breath

opend the windo near the egsit, took a deep breaf and took time

expel   until   were empty

to ecspel the air unti his lungs was empte. He looked out from the

ledge   hedge   embankment

window lej over the hege to the embancmunt.

smell

After all his hard work, he could smel success.

An Umbrella On The Summit

Sam wos talking to Jim abowt feeling unwel all of a suddun.

"It is discusting how uwell I feel. I suspeck eating too much cayk

is the culpit," he said. "I feel like I'll stay ill unles I buj myself and

suject my body to a gud walk upp the hil."

Jim said he wuld unlok the garage and unpark his climbing boots

and wait util Sam got redy Thay took the publick path to the sumit

of the locul hill. As the clock stuck three it started to rain on the

sunitt. Jim put his umbrelu up. Sam sed Jim was a good juj of the

weather.

An Umbrella On The Summit

was   about   unwell   sudden

Sam wos talking to Jim abowt feeling unwel all of a suddun.

disgusting   unwell   suspect   cake

"It is discusting how uwell I feel. I suspeck eating too much cayk

culprit   unless budge

is the culpit," he said. "I feel like I'll stay ill unles I buj myself and

subject   good   up   hill

suject my body to a gud walk upp the hil."

would unlock   unpack

Jim said he wuld unlok the garage and unpark his climbing boots

until   ready. They   public   summit

and wait util Sam got redy Thay took the publick path to the sumit

local   struck

of the locul hill. As the clock stuck three it started to rain on the

summit   umbrella   said   judge

sunitt. Jim put his umbrelu up. Sam sed Jim was a good juj of the

weather.

A Pocket Of Pickles

the jogger Holly ad Harry meet lives at the bak of town down a

tricke path full of pricles and nettles near the dusk pond. He has a

shop smac bang in the middle ov town that sells packits of brakets

and sockits for builders and also fishing takle and homemade

pickls

Some people corl him the pockit rokit as he is so qwik at

joggin. Some peple say he might get a speeding tiket for jogging

too fast!

Gus bought sum of the pickes but the top cam off in his jackit

pokit and the vinegar tricled down his leg. Yuck!

Level 2 – Activity 6 – 'ck'

A Pocket Of Pickles

The   and   met   back

the jogger Holly ad Harry meet lives at the bak of town down a

tricky   prickles   duck

tricke path full of pricles and nettles near the dusk pond. He has a

smack   of   packets brackets

shop smac bang in the middle ov town that sells packits of brakets

sockets   tackle

and sockits for builders and also fishing takle and homemade

pickles.

pickls

call   pocket rocket   quick

Some people corl him the pockit rokit as he is so qwik at

jogging   people   ticket

joggin. Some peple say he might get a speeding tiket for jogging

too fast!

some   pickles   came   jacket

Gus bought sum of the pickes but the top cam off in his jackit

pocket   trickled

pokit and the vinegar tricled down his leg. Yuck!

13

Sleepless After Coffee

There was a cold breez is the air and the rain was staring to freaz

and turn to sleer. Jim and Sam were out in the car when there was

a screetch of steal.

Sam sqeezed Jim's sleev. What was that? Say Sam. The weel had

came lose on a truck carrying cheez. Jim and Sam ugread the driver

had got seepy and hit the wal.

The driver woz okay but he had hit his nee in the cab and it was

beginning to bled. They managed to stop the bledding while Jim

gave him some coffe he had left in his flak.

"I think I'll have a sleeples night but thanks for helpin me, the driver

said gratefully.

Sleepless After Coffee

breeze in   starting   freeze

There was a cold breez is the air and the rain was staring to freaz

sleet

and turn to sleer. Jim and Sam were out in the car when there was

screech   steel

a screetch of steal.

squeezed   sleeve "   " said   wheel

Sam sqeezed Jim's sleev. What was that? Say Sam. The weel had

come loose   cheese   agreed

came lose on a truck carrying cheez. Jim and Sam ugread the driver

sleepy   wall

had got seepy and hit the wal.

was   knee

The driver woz okay but he had hit his nee in the cab and it was

bleed   bleeding

beginning to bled. They managed to stop the bledding while Jim

coffee   flask

gave him some coffe he had left in his flak.

sleepless   thanks   helping   "

"I think I'll have a sleeples night but thanks for helpin me, the driver

said gratefully.

The Crooked Blooms

It was 12 noone and the wether had tirned gloome and coowl. Ann and Sue wer quite moode and both lookd full of dowm and glom.

The hoock on the wuden greenhouse door had worn smmooth and come loos. Sue felt foolsh as she should hav fixed it and now the grenhouse was not weatherprof.

"Aargh!" she boomd. Sue hopped all around the gardun like a kangro.

They were supposed to chose some flowers for the flower snow.

Looking into the greenhouse, thay coud see that the wind had blown in and every bloome was crookd and bent.

The Crooked Blooms

noon   weather   turned gloomy   cool

It was 12 noone and the wether had tirned gloome and coowl. Ann

were   moody   looked   doom   gloom

and Sue wer quite moode and both lookd full of dowm and glom.

hook   wooden   smooth

The hoock on the wuden greenhouse door had worn smmooth and

loose   foolish   have

come loos. Sue felt foolsh as she should hav fixed it and now the

greenhouse   weatherproof

grenhouse was not weatherprof.

boomed   garden

"Aargh!" she boomd. Sue hopped all around the gardun like a

kangaroo

kangro.

choose   show

They were supposed to chose some flowers for the flower snow.

they could

Looking into the greenhouse, thay coud see that the wind had blown

bloom   crooked

in and every bloome was crookd and bent.

The Carpet Department

The wether had turned artik cold and sam had taken Gran to the

indor market so she didn't come to any arm in the darc She

needed a karton of milk and some pasnips. She put the parsnis in the

compatmunt of her trolley.

they passed an artis who was drawing harmles funny car tunes of

people.

Gran sai, "Before we depaat I want to look in the carrpit

deeparment as I saw a skarlut rug that would be just rite for the

hall."

Sam replied that he didn' mind. He just wonted Gran to get home

unarmed with no skars from falling over in the darknes.

The Carpet Department

weather   arctic   Sam

The wether had turned artik cold and sam had taken Gran to the

indoor market   harm   dark.

indor market so she didn't come to any arm in the darc She

carton   parsnips   parsnips

needed a karton of milk and some pasnips. She put the parsnis in the

compartment

compatmunt of her trolley.

They   artist   harmless   cartoons

they passed an artis who was drawing harmles funny car tunes of

people.

said   depart   carpet

Gran sai, "Before we depaat I want to look in the carrpit

department   scarlet   right

deeparment as I saw a skarlut rug that would be just rite for the

hall."

didn't   wanted

Sam replied that he didn' mind. He just wonted Gran to get home

unharmed   scars   darkness

unarmed with no skars from falling over in the darknes.

A Sharp Shock

Sam had finish his lunch. He'd had masht potato and shrims. He

needed to go to the shed to sharpun some tools and finsh putting

some varnis on some wodcarvings he had made.

Suddenly, there was a shap fash and a krash. The shed started

shaykin and the shelves shooc and shuderd. Pots and tins crasht to

the floor and the varnsh splased everywhere.

Sam did not hav a clue what happened. He was scared and in shok

when it had finised. Later, there was a newsflas that said their has

been a freek lightening stom and an earthkwake.

A Sharp Shock

finished   mashed   shrimps

Sam had finish his lunch. He'd had masht potato and shrims. He

              sharpen   finish

needed to go to the shed to sharpun some tools and finsh putting

    varnish   woodcarvings

some varnis on some wodcarvings he had made.

              sharp flash   crash

Suddenly, there was a shap fash and a krash. The shed started

shaking   shook   shuddered   crashed

shaykin and the shelves shooc and shuderd. Pots and tins crasht to

          varnish splashed

the floor and the varnsh splased everywhere.

          have   happened   shock

Sam did not hav a clue what happened. He was scared and in shok

          finished   newsflash   there had

when it had finised. Later, there was a newsflas that said their has

    freak lightning storm   earthquake

been a freek lightening stom and an earthkwake.

Level 2 – Activity 11 – 'ch' – Chasing The Chimpanzee

Holly and Harry wanted a chanje so they were gone to the orchud to

pick sherries and chesnutz. The chilldrun began to chattr about how

much they cud charj Gran to buy the cheerys.

"I bet she sez we've got a cheak chaging her for them," Holly chucled

Harry shoutd, "I am the tree-climbing champyun, and clenshd his fist

in the hair.

Just as he was abut to clim the tree, Chery, Adam's wife appeared.

She works at the zoo, and was chasin a chimpansy. Holly and

Harry looked at each uther and were totaly spechles.

Level 2 – Activity 12 – 'th' – Third And Fourth

harry had an aritmetik test. he was thancfull it was the sevnth and last

test as he was sick of then He had neva revised for this lenth of time and

his head was thik wiv a fousand mathz facts. He thort he had done quite

well in the first second sickth and fif tests but wasn't too sure about the

thurd and forth tests.   He throwed his head back and rubed his eyes with

his thums as he had read withowt a break for ages. His throte was dry

and he was thirty so he go for a drinc.

Level 2 – Activity 11 – 'ch' – Chasing The Chimpanzee

                      change   *going*   *orchard*

Holly and Harry wanted a chanje so they were gone to the orchud to

    cherries   *chestnuts*   *children*   *chatter*

pick sherries and chesnutz. The chilldrun began to chattr about how

       could charge   *cherries*

much they cud charj Gran to buy the cheerys.

      says   *cheek charging*   *chuckled.*

"I bet she sez we've got a cheak chaging her for them," Holly chucled

    shouted   *champion "*   *clenched*

Harry shoutd, "I am the tree-climbing champyun, and clenshd his fist

      air

in the hair.

         about   *climb*   *Cherry*

Just as he was abut to clim the tree, Chery, Adam's wife appeared.

                    chasing chimpanzee

She works at the zoo, and was chasin a chimpansy. Holly and

               other   *totally speechless*

Harry looked at each uther and were totaly spechles.

Level 2 – Activity 12 – 'th' – Third And Fourth

Harry   *arithmetic*   *He*   *thankful*   *seventh*

harry had an aritmetik test. he was thancfull it was the sevnth and last

               them.   *never*   *length*

test as he was sick of then He had neva revised for this lenth of time and

      thick with thousand maths   *thought*

his head was thik wiv a fousand mathz facts. He thort he had done quite

       ,   , *sixth*   *fifth*

well in the first second sickth and fif tests but wasn't too sure about the

third   *fourth*   *threw*   *rubbed*

thurd and forth tests.   He throwed his head back and rubed his eyes with

   thumbs   *without*   *throat*

his thums as he had read withowt a break for ages. His throte was dry

    thirsty   *went*   *drink*

and he was thirty so he go for a drinc.

23

Level 2 – Activity 13 – 'or' – Doctor's Orders

Grandad hat to see the docktur as he'd had a bump on his forhed and it had made him snor mor The doctr's repourt was an impotant record as it infoumed Grandad that he was forrbiden to drive his motur car until special tabluts had been odered.

"We don't have them in stor here," said the docter, "but forgiv me, I'll have to ourder them befor you can drive again You'll hav to use public tran sport but maybe you can ecsplor some knew places on the train? Don't stand to close to the edge of the platfom though.

Level 2 – Activity 14 – 'a' – A Strange Place

Ann had been gave the wrong wajis and had sent a pryvit email messige to the wayge clerk to say they had made a misteak. Ther needed to be a chaynje on the payges of her wag slip. It wuz strainge becoz she had never had too fase the problem befor. It was a discrase as it took an ayj to make the chainges.

She had to go to a new spays, a plaice in the basment of the offis under the pavmunt. She went safly down the steps and was pleasd to see a choclat machine in the foyer, but it was damiged.

Level 2 – Activity 13 – 'or' – Doctor's Orders

had   doctor   forehead

Grandad hat to see the docktur as he'd had a bump on his forhed and it

snore more.   doctor's report   important

had made him snor mor The doctr's repourt was an impotant record as

informed   forbidden   motor

it infoumed Grandad that he was forrbiden to drive his motur car until

tablets   ordered

special tabluts had been odered.

store   doctor   forgive

"We don't have them in stor here," said the docter, "but forgiv me, I'll

order   before   .   have

have to ourder them befor you can drive again You'll hav to use public

transport   explore   new

tran sport but maybe you can ecsplor some knew places on the train?

too   platform   "

Don't stand to close to the edge of the platfom though.

Level 2 – Activity 14 – 'a' – A Strange Place

given   wages   private   message

Ann had been gave the wrong wajis and had sent a pryvit email messige

wage   mistake There

to the wayge clerk to say they had made a misteak. Ther needed to be a

change   pages   wage   was strange because

chaynje on the payges of her wag slip. It wuz strainge becoz she had

to face   before   disgrace   age

never had too fase the problem befor. It was a discrase as it took an ayj

changes

to make the chainges.

space   place   basement   office

She had to go to a new spays, a plaice in the basment of the offis under

pavement   safely   pleased

the pavmunt. She went safly down the steps and was pleasd to see a

chocolate   damaged

choclat machine in the foyer, but it was damiged.

25

Level 2 – Activity 15 – 'i-e' – The Ice Cream Invite

Sam and Jim had day off from the offis as new wiyres for the fyre alarms were rekwired. They quiet like the idea of going to the golf course to practis and get some advise from the professional golfer there. As they arrivd a plees car passt the gates with its sirun going but sam and jim took no notis.

They had to higher some clubs and a bucket of ninete balls but the prise was cheep The golf pro told Jim to moov his hand over the club as he had sliysd the ball twiyce. Afterwards, he invyted them innside is cream.

Level 2 – Activity 16 – 'o-e' – Smoking Clothes

Gus was howm alowne. He had just finished foning Sam. They spowke about booking a otel or a mowtel as they were hopin to get away for a few days. He whent into the garden to water the tomatos and potatos. Usually he was hoples at growing tomatows but he hopped to have a good crop this year. He had a hole basket of cloths two peg out but the fone rang again. When he came back out the clothz were smokig next door had lit a fire and a spark had jumpt ovur the fence. The smowk made Gus chok but by a strowk of luck the ose was still attached to the tap so he put the fire out kwickly

Level 2 – Activity 15 – 'i-e' – The Ice Cream Invite

        a   *office*   *wires*   *fire*

Sam and Jim had day off from the offis as new wiyres for the fyre alarms

    required   *quite liked*

were rekwired. They quiet like the idea of going to the golf course to

practise   *advice*

practis and get some advise from the professional golfer there. As they

arrived police   *passed*   *siren*   *Sam*   *Jim*

arrivd a plees car passt the gates with its sirun going but sam and jim

      notice

took no notis.

       hire   *ninety*   *price*

They had to higher some clubs and a bucket of ninete balls but the prise

  cheap.   *move*

was cheep The golf pro told Jim to moov his hand over the club as he had

sliced   *twice*   *invited*   *inside for ice*

sliysd the ball twiyce. Afterwards, he invyted them innside is cream.

Level 2 – Activity 16 – 'o-e' – Smoking Clothes

      home alone   *phoning*   *spoke*

Gus was howm alowne. He had just finished foning Sam. They spowke

       hotel   *motel*   *hoping*

about booking a otel or a mowtel as they were hopin to get away for

          went   *tomatoes*   *potatoes*

a few days. He whent into the garden to water the tomatos and potatos.

     hopeless   *tomatoes*   *hoped*

Usually he was hoples at growing tomatows but he hopped to have a

               whole   *clothes to*

good crop this year. He had a hole basket of cloths two peg out but the

phone   *clothes*   *smoking.* Next

fone rang again. When he came back out the clothz were smokig next

               jumped over   *smoke*

door had lit a fire and a spark had jumpt ovur the fence. The smowk

    choke   *stroke*   *hose*

made Gus chok but by a strowk of luck the ose was still attached to the

             quickly.

tap so he put the fire out kwickly

Level 2 – Activity 17 – 'u-e' – Ann's True Rules

ann lived a pyure and simple life as a rool. She refoosd to argu with

anyone who akused her of doing something she hadnt done, but it did

make her fyum.

It amyewsed her wen people continud to yuse any excuce to try and injur

her feeling. She olways saw the big picher and remained tru to herself

and her rools. Some peple just did not have a clew and she was shure

she would contunu her good life in the fewture.

Level 2 – Activity 18 – 'ai' – Trail Training

Adam was in traning agen. He was trale and mountin-running agenst the

clock mainle, and he had lost weight from his waste. He wonted Cheery

to run with him but she was like a snayl at running. Cherrey was lerning

to sale a bote though, so wasn't a complete sporting failyer and she had

picked up saling qickly.

Adam had got an injury that give him a lot of payn which needed first-

ade but he wasn't afrayd. Even thoug it was very paneful, he remaned

hopeful he wuld stay fit for the time-trial.

Level 2 – Activity 17 – 'u-e' – Ann's True Rules

Ann   pure   rule   refused   argue

ann lived a pyure and simple life as a rool. She refoosd to argu with

accused   hadn't

anyone who akused her of doing something she hadnt done, but it did

fume

make her fyum.

amused   when   continued   use   excuse   injure

It amyewsed her wen people continud to yuse any excuce to try and injur

feelings   always   picture   true

her feeling. She olways saw the big picher and remained tru to herself

rules   people   clue   sure

and her rools. Some peple just did not have a clew and she was shure

continue   future

she would contunu her good life in the fewture.

Level 2 – Activity 18 – 'ai' – Trail Training

training again   trail   mountain   against

Adam was in traning agen. He was trale and mountin-running agenst the

mainly   waist   wanted Cherry

clock mainle, and he had lost weight from his waste. He wonted Cheery

snail   Cherry   learning

to run with him but she was like a snayl at running. Cherrey was lerning

sail boat   failure

to sale a bote though, so wasn't a complete sporting failyer and she had

sailing quickly

picked up saling qickly.

gave   pain

Adam had got an injury that give him a lot of payn which needed first-

aid   afraid   though   painful   remained

ade but he wasn't afrayd. Even thoug it was very paneful, he remaned

would

hopeful he wuld stay fit for the time-trial.

Level 2 – Activity 19 – 'oa' – The Roar Of The Coastline

Cherry had a goall as she approched her birthday. She wanted to sail part of the coatline. she had to coaks Adam to go with her and he moned that he olways got a sore throte when he went to sea She told him to stop moning and groning.

"You'll be able to boste you've sailed the cowst in a bote, she said.

Cherry checked with the coastgard that the ors were loded abord and the lifebote floted with a full lowd, but they were shure they wouldn't have a man ovubord. They got their cotes from the clokeroom and left.

Level 2 – Activity 20 – 'ir' – Squirm At The Circus

The sircus was in town for the furst time in ages. It was there for therty dayz. Grandad had confurmd Holly and Harri wer booked to see it on the fird night. Holly did a twerl she was so exsited.

The Big Top was a big sirclar tent which was furmly secured to the ground wiv thirtene big ropes and pegs The clowns came in and did a sircuit around the sir cumference of the ring on funny bikes. One caused a stur when he twirld a wriggly rubber worm arownd his head which made poeple squrm. Another one spun around in sircul and squurted people with water. It great fun.

30

Level 2 – Activity 19 – 'oa' – The Roar Of The Coastline

goal   approached

Cherry had a goall as she approched her birthday. She wanted to sail part

coastline She   coax   moaned

of the coatline. she had to coaks Adam to go with her and he moned

always   throat

that he olways got a sore throte when he went to sea She told him to

moaning   groaning

stop moning and groning.

boast   coast   boat,"

"You'll be able to boste you've sailed the cowst in a bote, she said.

coastguard   oars   loaded aboard

Cherry checked with the coastgard that the ors were loded abord and the

lifeboat floated   load   sure

lifebote floted with a full lowd, but they were shure they wouldn't have a

overboard   coats   cloakroom

man ovubord. They got their cotes from the clokeroom and left.

Level 2 – Activity 20 – 'ir' – Squirm At The Circus

circus   first   thirty

The sircus was in town for the furst time in ages. It was there for therty

days   confirmed   Harry were

dayz. Grandad had confurmd Holly and Harri wer booked to see it on the

third   twirl   excited

fird night. Holly did a twerl she was so exsited.

circular   firmly

The Big Top was a big sirclar tent which was furmly secured to the

with thirteen

ground wiv thirtene big ropes and pegs The clowns came in and did a

circuit   circumference

sircuit around the sir cumference of the ring on funny bikes. One caused

stir   twirled   around

a stur when he twirld a wriggly rubber worm arownd his head which

people squirm   a circle   squirted

made poeple squrm. Another one spun around in sircul and squurted

was   !

people with water. It great fun.

Level 2 – Activity 21 – 'ou' – The Council Fountain

the cownty counsul were very prowd. They were abou to anounse that the public acounts had a few thousund pownds to spend on something nise for the town. This umount woz due to sownd and stoutt managing of the money saved on the upkeep the paths that suround the montain

"It is ower intention to put a fowntin in the middle of the new rondubout that is being built in the southe of the town. The fontain will go off every our on the our, a spokesman said.

Level 2 – Activity 22 – 'ea' – Bad Gears?

Jim had been meening to check over his car as it appered to be overhating.

He had his work jeens on and was leenin into the engine loking a the geerboks With the change in the seasuns it could easly be that he needed to put some special gere oil in but that wasnt it. he was getting a bit tried and reely weery of trying to find te problem.

"Aha!" he cried. He couold see a leef under a pipe, then found a bunch of leeves blocking the pipe. thay were eazy to pull out and after he had done that the heting problem disupered

Level 2 – Activity 21 – 'ou' – The Council Fountain

The county council proud about announce
the cownty counsul were very prowd. They were abou to anounse that

accounts thousand pounds
the public acounts had a few thousund pownds to spend on something

nice amount was sound stout
nise for the town. This umount woz due to sownd and stoutt managing

of surround mountain.
of the money saved on the upkeep the paths that suround the montain

our fountain roundabout
"It is ower intention to put a fowntin in the middle of the new rondubout

south fountain
that is being built in the southe of the town. The fontain will go off every

hour hour"
our on the our, a spokesman said.

Level 2 – Activity 22 – 'ea' – Bad Gears?

meaning appeared
Jim had been meening to check over his car as it appered to be

overheating
overhating.

jeans leaning looking at
He had his work jeens on and was leenin into the engine loking a the

gearbox. seasons easily
geerboks With the change in the seasuns it could easly be that he

gear wasn't He
needed to put some special gere oil in but that wasnt it. he was getting a

tired really weary the
bit tried and reely weery of trying to find te problem.

could leaf
"Aha!" he cried. He couold see a leef under a pipe, then found a bunch of

leaves They easy
leeves blocking the pipe. thay were eazy to pull out and after he had

heating disappeared.
done that the heting problem disupered

33

Level 2 – Activity 23 – 'ur' – The Furniture Burglary

There have been a burgulary at the fernichure store. there was more than one birglur and they must have both been very burle as they took an adsurd amount of furnture and kurtins. It were a suprise nobody heard the disturbans. There was not a murmer

The chief of police called an urjent meeting to pirsew the culprits. "It takes burglars of great pirpus not to distuerb anyone," he said. "I want you to sirvay the north subburb and then the south suberb Keep a look out for eny houses with new curtins and any sirplus gardun furniture."

Level 2 – Activity 24 – 'aw' – Awful Drawing

Grandad had taken up droring. He had olways secretly wanted to be a good draw. His first attempts to drew were orful. He had a very rawe, orkwud, sprorling style but the art teecher was awflly nice to him

After class, Grandad thawd some prorns and strawbrys and cream for tea. Grandad asked Gran if he could dror her.

Gran agreed. "But don't make my jor look too big!" Gran had laid down the lore. When he showd Gran finished drawing she started to ball.

"That is so bad it should be unlawful. I ought to call my loyer!"

Grandad smiled orkwudly.

Level 2 – Activity 23 – 'ur' – The Furniture Burglary

had   burglary   furniture   There

There have been a burgulary at the fernichure store. there was more than

burglar   burly

one birglur and they must have both been very burle as they took an

absurd   furniture   curtains   was   surprise

adsurd amount of furnture and kurtins. It were a suprise nobody heard

disturbance   murmur.

the disturbans. There was not a murmer

urgent   pursue

The chief of police called an urjent meeting to pirsew the culprits. "It

purpose   disturb

takes burglars of great pirpus not to distuerb anyone," he said. "I want

survey   suburb   suburb.

you to sirvay the north subburb and then the south suberb Keep a look

any   curtains   surplus garden

out for eny houses with new curtins and any sirplus gardun furniture."

Level 2 – Activity 24 – 'aw' – Awful Drawing

drawing   always

Grandad had taken up droring. He had olways secretly wanted to be a

drawer   draw   awful   raw

good draw. His first attempts to drew were orful. He had a very rawe,

awkward, sprawling   teacher   awfully   .

orkwud, sprorling style but the art teecher was awflly nice to him

thawed   prawns   strawberries

After class, Grandad thawd some prorns and strawbrys and cream for

draw

tea. Grandad asked Gran if he could dror her.

jaw

Gran agreed. "But don't make my jor look too big!" Gran had laid down

law   showed   the   bawl

the lore. When he showd Gran finished drawing she started to ball.

unlawful   lawyer

"That is so bad it should be unlawful. I ought to call my loyer!"

awkwardly

Grandad smiled orkwudly.

Level 2 – Activity 25 – 'oi' – The Unavoidable Ointment

The local church cwire and the male voyse kwire needed to apoint

substitute khoir-masters the apointmunts were unuvoydabl as both

con duc tors had got food-posoning and thay couldn't avoyd needing the

toylet evry five minutes!

The doctor had given them some oyntmunt wrapped in fol and a special

oyl to help with the 'moistur' problem they were also disupointid to find

that raising their voyses was to be avoydid at all costs, which obviously

was a sore poynt.

Level 2 – Activity 26 – 'er' – The Uncertain Prime Minister

Holly and Harry were at the sopermarkit with grandad getting groserys.

the growcers shop was shut while he had an opurashun on his nervus system.

Next door, the travel ajent had discounts on sertun holidays to

Switzurland, jursey and jermuny.

"Have you been to Jirmany, Grandad?" Holly asked.

"I sirtunly have. I remembur it well although I'm unsurtun of the exact

date. It very inturestin as the Prime minster was a passinjer on the same

plane and he could not undrstan how to oprayt the seet-belts and could

not control his angur, Grandad laughed loudly.

Level 2 – Activity 25 – 'oi' – The Unavoidable Ointment

choir   voice choir   appoint

The local church cwire and the male voyse kwire needed to apoint

choir   . The appointments   unavoidable

substitute khoir-masters the apointmunts were unuvoydabl as both

conductors   poisoning   they   avoid

con duc tors had got food-posoning and thay couldn't avoyd needing the

toilet every

toylet evry five minutes!

ointment   foil

The doctor had given them some oyntmunt wrapped in fol and a special

oil   moisture   . They   disappointed

oyl to help with the 'moistur' problem they were also disupointid to find

voices   avoided

that raising their voyses was to be avoydid at all costs, which obviously

point

was a sore poynt.

Level 2 – Activity 26 – 'er' – The Uncertain Prime Minister

supermarket   Grandad   groceries

Holly and Harry were at the sopermarkit with grandad getting groserys.

The grocer's   operation   nervous

the growcers shop was shut while he had an opurashun on his nervus system.

agent   certain

Next door, the travel ajent had discounts on sertun holidays to

Switzerland, Jersey   Germany

Switzurland, jursey and jermuny.

Germany

"Have you been to Jirmany, Grandad?" Holly asked.

certainly   remember   uncertain

"I sirtunly have. I remembur it well although I'm unsurtun of the exact

was   interesting   Minister   passenger

date. It very inturestin as the Prime minster was a passinjer on the same

understand   operate   seat

plane and he could not undrstan how to oprayt the seet-belts and could

anger"

not control his angur, Grandad laughed loudly.

Level 2 – Activity 27 – 'al' – Naturally Musical

gus was a natrul musician and he was unusaly good on the floot and had

continuly improved He had olso started learning the drums oltho

he was olmost eqally as good. He was olwiz practising but he made such

an olmitey racket it was criminul. He needed his anewal hearing check-up

at the centrul hopsitul but they had to oltur the day of the appointment.

when she called, the lady on the fone said, Change to Thursday

Gus said, "No I'm OK thanks, Ive olredy had three cups of tea oltugether."

Level 2 – Activity 28 – 'ea' – short 'e' The Healthy Headmistress

The wether had been getting stedly worse as Holly got reddy to go to the

gym. she bumped into the hedmisres. ooh, stedy Miss!" Holly said.

"Im sorry Holly, I was looking straight ahed and didn't see you. I've

got a bad hedake and I'm trying to get helthy. normally it's a plesure to

come training a they have such a welth of machines to mesure your elth

here but this hedake thretuns to make me unstedy."

Holly replied, "Miss, why don't you have a rest and get swetty another

day? You'll be light as a fethr in no time."

Miss said, Thats a good idea Holly, you're a treasure, but remember,

ladies don't swet, we glow."

Level 2 – Activity 27 – 'al' – Naturally Musical

Gus natural   unusually   flute

gus was a natrul musician and he was unusaly good on the floot and had

continually   .   also   although

continuly improved He had olso started learning the drums oltho

  almost equally   always

he was olmost eqally as good. He was olwiz practising but he made such

  almighty   criminal   annual

an olmitey racket it was criminul. He needed his anewal hearing check-up

  central hospital   alter

at the centrul hopsitul but they had to oltur the day of the appointment.

When   phone "   ."

when she called, the lady on the fone said, Change to Thursday

      I've already   altogether

Gus said, "No I'm OK thanks, Ive olredy had three cups of tea oltugether."

Level 2 – Activity 28 – 'ea' – short 'e' The Healthy Headmistress

 weather   steadily   ready

The wether had been getting stedly worse as Holly got reddy to go to the

 She   headmistress "Ooh steady

gym. she bumped into the hedmisres. ooh, stedy Miss!" Holly said.

I'm   ahead

"Im sorry Holly, I was looking straight ahed and didn't see you. I've

  headache   healthy Normally pleasure

got a bad hedake and I'm trying to get helthy. normally it's a plesure to

   as   wealth   measure health

come training a they have such a welth of machines to mesure your elth

  headache threatens   unsteady

here but this hedake thretuns to make me unstedy."

             sweaty

Holly replied, "Miss, why don't you have a rest and get swetty another

     feather

day? You'll be light as a fethr in no time."

 "That's   treasure

Miss said, Thats a good idea Holly, you're a treasure, but remember,

  sweat

ladies don't swet, we glow."

Level 2 – Activity 29 – 'ow' – Power After The Shower

Harry had been in the gardun planting seeds with a new powur trowl. The powr trowul plugs in to the powurr supply and makes the soil easier to dig. the gardening had made him drowzy so he was allowd to go to the gym for a quick swim In the showr room there was a rowde man flicking his towl at peple and throwing talcum powdur around.

Just then a big powrfull man stood towring over the bully. We don't ulow that in here! boomed the man. The bully quickly became a cowud and left.

Level 2 – Activity 30 – silent letters – The Wrong Answer

Harry and Holly ofn went to the museum for an our or too.They new the gide and oftn had tea and biskits with the gard. He was a funny giy and they liked to lisn to his stories of famus gests that had visited the bilding.

The gide was take some very yung children around, and one poked his tung out behind her back. She asked did anyone no wich year they began to bild the museum.

"a vage gess, 1926?" somebody said. "No, that is the rong anser," replied the guid. "It was 1927, onist. You were only one year out."

Level 2 – Activity 29 – 'ow' – Power After The Shower

gardun   power trowel

Harry had been in the gardun planting seeds with a new powur trowl. The

power trowel   power

powr trowul plugs in to the powurr supply and makes the soil easier to

The   drowsy   allowed

dig. the gardening had made him drowzy so he was allowd to go to the

.   shower   rowdy

gym for a quick swim In the showr room there was a rowde man flicking

towel   people   powder

his towl at peple and throwing talcum powdur around.

powerful   towering   "   allow

Just then a big powrfull man stood towring over the bully. We don't ulow

"   coward

that in here! boomed the man. The bully quickly became a cowud and

left.

Level 2 – Activity 30 – silent letters – The Wrong Answer

often   hour   two   knew

Harry and Holly ofn went to the museum for an our or too. They new the

guide   often   biscuits   guard   guy

gide and oftn had tea and biskits with the gard. He was a funny giy and

listen   famous guests   building

they liked to lisn to his stories of famus gests that had visited the bilding.

guide   taking   young

The gide was take some very yung children around, and one poked his

tongue   know which

tung out behind her back. She asked did anyone no wich year they began

build

to bild the museum.

A vague guess   wrong answer

"a vage gess, 1926?" somebody said. "No, that is the rong anser,"

guide   honest

replied the guid. "It was 1927, onist. You were only one year out."

41

Level 2 – Activity 31 – 'a' (ar) – The Dance Trance

arnty Ann was in a trans. She had been to a danc lesson where the

teacher had demarndid thay prans about for harf an hour. Her carf was

sore arfter but she stayed carm.

"Ive got just the arnser to stop the pain advarnsing. I'll farsn an ice-

pack on when get home," she sed. Before she put the pak on she poured

some soothing barm she had bought in Frans into her pam and rubbed it

in. Before she sat down she glarnsd outside. It was overcarst.

One advarntij of having a bad carff is she had to rest up. Just then the

doorbel rang. It was sue with rasbry tart and cream.

Level 2 – Activity 32 – Endings – Jealous And Envious

Grandad was feeling a bit misrabl as he had sudnly been getting some

invisbl aches that were horbly painfl. It was probly arthritis and was not

a surprise to be truful for sumeone of his vintage. Thankfly he had a

wonderfly elpful famly and he was abl to handl the trembls and shayks

that come with old age. He had lived a simpl life and was doing sensibl

exercises to help himself.

It is very probabl that he will live to be a hundred, which is wondufl.

Level 2 – Activity 31 – 'a' (ar) – The Dance Trance

Aunty   trance   dance

arnty Ann was in a trans. She had been to a danc lesson where the

demanded they prance   half   calf

teacher had demarndid thay prans about for harf an hour. Her carf was

after   calm

sore arfter but she stayed carm.

I've   answer   advancing   fasten

"Ive got just the arnser to stop the pain advarnsing. I'll farsn an ice-

I   said   pack

pack on when get home," she sed. Before she put the pak on she poured

balm   France   palm

some soothing barm she had bought in Frans into her pam and rubbed it

glanced   overcast

in. Before she sat down she glarnsd outside. It was overcarst.

advantage   calf

One advarntij of having a bad carff is she had to rest up. Just then the

doorbell   Sue   raspberry

doorbel rang. It was sue with rasbry tart and cream.

Level 2 – Activity 32 – Endings – Jealous And Envious

miserable   suddenly

Grandad was feeling a bit misrabl as he had sudnly been getting some

invisible   horribly painful   probably

invisbl aches that were horbly painfl. It was probly arthritis and was not

truthful   someone   Thankfully

a surprise to be truful for sumeone of his vintage. Thankfly he had a

wonderfully helpful family   able   handle   trembles   shakes

wonderfly elpful famly and he was abl to handl the trembls and shayks

simple   sensible

that come with old age. He had lived a simpl life and was doing sensibl

exercises to help himself.

probable   wonderful

It is very probabl that he will live to be a hundred, which is wondufl.

43

Level 2 – Activity 33 – 'au' – The Automobile Auction

Sam and Jim wer at the ortomobile awkshun looking at cars for Jim's

dorter. Her old car had cawt fire outside the lawndry in Awgust becoz it

had developd an electrical folt They wanted to make shure the new car

was not fawlty. There were people from everywhere at the arction.

They met an Ostrian and an Ostralian who had a horlage business and

needed some more vans

They larfed at the state of some of the cars but they all got foltless new

autos in the end.

Afterwards they had some collieflour cheese and sosij with brown sors.

Level 2 – Activity 34 – More Endings – Jealous And Envious

Granda was a little nervus and ankshus about his admisshun to hospital

The doctors were suspishus of a lump on leg but they didn't think it

was serous. The doctors had had a diskushn with Grandad and he had

givn them permishn to examin his leg as the doctors were curyous as to

what it was. Grandad wos in good spirits when sam visited and said,

"The food is delishus, the nurses are tremendus, the doctus are marvlus."

Sam was very envyus and jelus and shouted, Nurse, I'd like to be ill please!

"Dont be ridiclus," Grandad smiled.

Level 2 – Activity 33 – 'au' – The Automobile Auction

were   automobile auction

Sam and Jim wer at the ortomobile awkshun looking at cars for Jim's

daughter   caught   laundry August because

dorter. Her old car had cawt fire outside the lawndry in Awgust becoz it

developed   fault.   sure

had developd an electrical folt They wanted to make shure the new car

faulty   auction

was not fawlty. There were people from everywhere at the arction.

Austrian   Australian   haulage

They met an Ostrian and an Ostralian who had a horlage business and

needed some more vans

laughed   faultless

They larfed at the state of some of the cars but they all got foltless new

autos in the end.

cauliflower   sausage   sauce

Afterwards they had some collieflour cheese and sosij with brown sors.

Level 2 – Activity 34 – More Endings – Jealous And Envious

Grandad   nervous anxious   admission

Granda was a little nervus and ankshus about his admisshun to hospital

suspicious   his

The doctors were suspishus of a lump on leg but they didn't think it

serious   discussion

was serous. The doctors had had a diskushn with Grandad and he had

given permission examine   curious

givn them permishn to examin his leg as the doctors were curyous as to

was   Sam

what it was. Grandad wos in good spirits when sam visited and said,

delicious   tremendous doctors marvellous

"The food is delishus, the nurses are tremendus, the doctus are marvlus."

envious jealous   "   "

Sam was very envyus and jelus and shouted, Nurse, I'd like to be ill please!

Don't ridiculous

"Dont be ridiclus," Grandad smiled.

Level 2 – Activity 35 – Letters saying their own name – The Silent Violin

Holly's skool had a sumer fair a while agow. The postur was on the big

notis board on the traffic ilund and in the libry. There were all sorts

of stalls selling things. There was a motur-byke, an old bisikl with onle

one weel, an even older trysikl, a set of golf iruns and a steam iyun.

There was a wynde-up gost toy that lifted its arms up and made a 'woo'

sound and one stall had a dimund brooch that somebody finly bought fot

a lot of money. Another stall sold potaytoe and tumarto soup.

Out of now where, Holly notissd something she wanted.

she bought a silunt vilin. Yes, it had no strings!

Level 2 – Activity 35 – Letters saying their own name – The Silent Violin

school   summer   ago   poster

Holly's skool had a sumer fair a while agow. The postur was on the big

notice   island   library

notis board on the traffic ilund and in the libry. There were all sorts

motor-bike   bicycle   only

of stalls selling things. There was a motur-byke, an old bisikl with onle

wheel   tricycle   irons   iron

one weel, an even older trysikl, a set of golf iruns and a steam iyun.

wind   ghost

There was a wynde-up gost toy that lifted its arms up and made a 'woo'

diamond   finally   for

sound and one stall had a dimund brooch that somebody finly bought fot

potato   tomato

a lot of money. Another stall sold potaytoe and tumarto soup.

nowhere   noticed

Out of now where, Holly notissd something she wanted.

She   silent violin

she bought a silunt vilin. Yes, it had no strings!

47

Teaching points – Page 2

High Frequency Words – could, anyone.
Vocabulary – satchel, badger, admit. 'tch' family.

Example words from SME* books – VB* Textbook Level 2 Page 2 FWP* Pages 2-5	act	gigantic	plastic	admit	drag
	fact	badger	satchel	perhaps	plastic
	catch	scratch	canal	family	
	snatch	latch	angry	attacked	

*SME = Spelling Made Easy.   *VB = Violet Brand.   *FWP = Fun With Phonics Books.

Teaching points – Page 4

High Frequency Words – walking, again, year.
Silent 'k' and soft 'g'.
Vocabulary – common – different meanings, contented, compliment, contradict & any others.

Example words from SME books – VB Textbook Level 2 Page 2 FWP Pages 2-5	common	spotted	comment	flopped	boss
	contented	jogger	spot	cross	loss
	contest	jog	knot	compliment	spotted
	promptly	glossy	knockout	contradict	

Teaching points – Page 6

High Frequency Words – there, their, only.
Prefixes - mis, mini, dis.
Vocabulary – district, distinct, ridge, wring, mishap. Also 'dge' pattern.

Example words from SME books – VB Textbook Level 2 Page 3 FWP Pages 2-5	tipped	distinct	ridge	mistake	minimum
	disco	fridge	wring	mishap	trip
	district	liquid	wrist	minicab	
	bridge	dripping	minibus	misprint	

Teaching points – Page 8

Vocabulary – hectic, expel, embankment, credit.
'ex' – as in out of/former.

Example words from SME books – VB Textbook Level 2 Page 4 FWP Pages 6-9	second	wxpected	expand	exit	hedge
	exam	credit	hectic	expel	embankment
	electricity	seven	spell	empty	smell
	electronics	text-books	edge	ledge	

Teaching points – Page 10

Prefix – 'un' – meaning 'opposite of'.
Vocabulary – suspect, culprit, budge, summit.

Example words from SME books – VB Textbook Level 2 Page 5 FWP Pages 6-9	unwell	culprit	unlock	struck
	sudden	until	unpack	unless
	disgusting	budge	public	umbrella
	suspect	subject	summit	judge

Teaching points – Page 12

Endings – 'et' and 'le' follows short vowel.
Vocabulary – tackle, brackets.

Example words from SME books – VB Textbook Level 2 Page 6 FWP Pages 10-13	back	smack	tackle	ticket
	tricky	packets	pickles	jacket
	prickles	brackets	pocket	quick
	duck	sockets	rocket	trickled

Teaching points – Page 14

Double 'ee' in breeze, freeze, squeeze.
Vocabulary – screech, sleet.

Example words from SME books – VB Textbook Level 2 Page 7 FWP Pages 10-13	breeze	steel	cheese	bleed
	freeze	squeeze	agreed	bleeding
	sleet	sleeve	sleepy	coffee
	screech	wheel	knee	sleepless

Teaching points – Page 16

'ed' endings – past tense.
'choose' vs 'loose' – 'z' and 's'.
Vocabulary – bloom, boomed, doom.

Example words from SME books – VB Textbook Level 2 Page 8 FWP Pages 10-13	noon	looked	wooden	proof	bloom
	gloomy	doom	smooth	boomed	crooked
	cool	gloom	loose	kangaroo	
	moody	hook	foolish	choose	

Teaching points – Page 18

Discuss similarities between 'compartment' and 'department' – also vocab.

Discuss 'arctic' (and Antarctic).

Vocabulary – arctic, scarlet.

Example words from SME books – VB Textbook Level 2 Page 9 FWP Pages 14-17	arctic	carton	harmless	department	darkness
	market	parsnips	cartoons	scarlet	
	harm	compartment	depart	unharmed	
	dark	artist	carpet	scars	

Teaching points – Page 20

'ed' past tense ending.

Vocabulary – shrimps (prawns), varnish, shudder.

Example words from SME books – VB Textbook Level 2 Page 10 FWP Pages 14-17	finished	finish	cash	crashed
	mashed	varnish	shaking	splashed
	shrimps	sharp	shook	shock
	sharpen	flash	shuddered	newsflash

Teaching points – Page 22

Cherry to cherries – plural = change the 'y' to an 'i' and add 'es'.

Take off 'e' and add 'ing' = charge – charging, also chase, change.

Example words from SME books – VB Textbook Level 2 Page 11 FWP Pages 18-21	change	children	champion	chasing
	orchard	chatter	clenched	chimpanzee
	cherries	charge	charging	chuckled
	chestnuts	cheek	Cherry	speechless

Teaching points – Page 22

'th' added to the end of some ordinal numbers.

Silent 'b' in thumb.

Example words from SME books – VB Textbook Level 2 Page 12 FWP Pages 18-21	arithmetic	thick	thought	third	throat
	thankful	with	sixth	threw	thirsty
	seventh	thousand	fifth	thumbs	
	length	maths	fourth	without	

Teaching points – Page 24

'Forehead' – discuss compound word.

'or' at end of eg doctor, motor sounds as a schwa – 'uh'.

Vocabulary – record = verb **and** noun, same with transport.

Example words from SME books – VB Textbook Level 2 Page 13 FWP Pages 18-21	doctor	report	forbidden	forgive	explore
	forehead	important	motor	order	platform
	snore	record	ordered	before	
	more	informed	store	transport	

Teaching points – Page 24

Discuss the soft 'g' and the soft 'c' in this exercise.

Suffix – 'ment' meaning 'condition of'.

Example words from SME books – VB Textbook Level 2 Page 14 FWP Pages 18-21	wages	mistake	face	space	safely
	private	change	disgrace	place	chocolate
	message	pages	age	basement	damaged
	wage	strange	changes	pavement	

Teaching points – Page 26

Soft 'c' in the 'ice' family.

Discuss the sound/spelling of 'ire' vs eg tyre, higher.

Example words from SME books – VB Textbook Level 2 Page 15 FWP Pages 22-25	office	quite	arrived	hire	twice
	wire	liked	police	ninety	invited
	fire	practice	siren	price	inside
	required	advice	notice	sliced	ice cream

Teaching points – Page 26

Take off 'e' and add 'ing' – hope, phone, smoke.

'Hopeless' – suffix 'less' means 'without'.

Vocabulary – motel, whole, choke, hose.

Example words from SME books – VB Textbook Level 2 Page 16 FWP Pages 26-29	home	hotel	potatoes	clothes	stroke
	alone	motel	hopeless	to	choke
	phoning	hoping	hoped	smoking	hose
	spoke	tomatoes	whole	smoke	phone

Teaching points – Page 28

Point out difference between 'pure' and 'sure' vs 'picture' and 'future' etc.

Vocabulary – accused, amused, excuse – noun and verb.

Example words from SME books – VB Textbook Level 2 Page 17 FWP Pages 26-29	pure	accused	excuse	rules	future
	rule	fume	injure	clue	
	refused	amused	picture	sure	
	argue	continued	true	continue	

Teaching points – Page 28

Discuss different phonemes e.g. 'ai' in training vs 'ai' in mountain.

Example words from SME books – VB Textbook Level 2 Page 18 FWP Pages 30-33	training	against	sail	first-aid
	again	mainly	failure	afraid
	trail	waist	sailing	painful
	mountain	snail	pain	remained

Teaching points – Page 30

Contractions – You'll = you will, you've = you have.

Coastguard = compound word with 'silent u'.

Vocabulary – approach, coax, boast.

Example words from SME books – VB Textbook Level 2 Page 19 FWP Pages 30-33	goal	moaned	boast	loaded	overboard
	approached	throat	coast	aboard	coats
	coastline	moaning	coastguard	floated	cloakroom
	coax	groaning	oars	load	boat

Teaching points – Page 30

Discuss 'cir' – circle, circuit, circular, circumference all to do with 'round'.

Vocabulary – confirm, circumference, squirm.

Example words from SME books – VB Textbook Level 2 Page 20 FWP Pages 30-33	circus	third	firmly	stir	squirted
	first	twirl	thirteen	twirled	
	thirty	excited	circuit	squirm	
	confirmed	circular	circumference	circle	

Teaching points – Page 32

Point out double consonants in 'announce', 'accounts' and 'surround'.

Revise definitions of nouns.

Example words from SME books – VB Textbook Level 2 Page 21 FWP Pages 34-37	county	announce	amount	mountain	our
	council	accounts	sound	fountain	hour
	proud	thousand	stout	roundabout	
	about	pounds	surround	south	

Teaching points – Page 32

Endings – easy-easily, leaf-leaves, real-really.

Example words from SME books – VB Textbook Level 2 Page 22 FWP Pages 34-37	meaning	leaning	gear	leaves
	appeared	gearbox	really	easy
	overheating	seasons	weary	heating
	jeans	easily	leaf	disappeared

Teaching points – Page 34

Look at 'y' turning 'burglar' into 'burglary'.

Vocabulary – burly, absurd, murmur, pursue, survey, suburb, surplus.

Example words from SME books – VB Textbook Level 2 Page 23 FWP Pages 34-37	burglary	absurd	murmur	disturb
	furniture	curtains	urgent	survey
	burglar	surprise	pursue	suburb
	burly	disturbance	purpose	surplus

Teaching points – Page 34

When 'ful' is last syllable, only one 'l'.

Vocabulary – raw, sprawling, thaw.

Example words from SME books – VB Textbook Level 2 Page 24 FWP Pages 38-41	drawing	raw	thawed	law
	drawer	awkward	prawns	lawyer
	draw	sprawling	strawberries	bawl
	awful	awfully	jaw	unlawful

Teaching points – Page 36

Vocabulary – appointments, (un)avoidable, moisture.

Discuss why 'moisture' is in inverted commas.

Example words from SME books – VB Textbook Level 2 Page 25 FWP Pages 38-41	choir	unavoidable	ointment	disappointed
	voice	poisoning	foil	voices
	appoint	avoid	oil	avoided
	appointments	toilet	moisture	point

Teaching points – Page 36

Discuss endings – -ate, -ous, -ent, -cise.

Look at Jersey, Germany and Switzerland on a map.

Talk about Prime Minister and other leaders.

Example words from SME books – VB Textbook Level 2 Page 26 FWP Pages 38-41	supermarket	nervous	Germany	interesting	operate
	groceries	certain	certainly	Prime Minister	anger
	grocer	Switzerland	remember	passenger	
	operation	Jersey	uncertain	understand	

Teaching points – Page 38

Point out 'al' prefix sounds as 'ol', 'al' suffix sounds as 'ul'.

Double the 'l' when adding 'y'.

Vocabulary – annual, continual, alter.

Example words from SME books – VB Textbook Level 2 Page 27 FWP Pages 42-45	natural	although	almighty	hospital
	unusually	almost	criminal	alter
	continually	equally	annual	already
	also	always	central	altogether

Teaching points – Page 38

Steady – steadily.

Treasure, measure, pleasure.

Example words from SME books – VB Textbook Level 2 Page 28 FWP Pages 42-45	weather	steady	pleasure	threatens	treasure
	steadily	ahead	wealth	unsteady	sweat
	ready	headache	measure	sweaty	
	headmistress	healthy	health	feather	

Teaching points – Page 40

'el' soundings as 'ul' at the end of a word.

Vocabulary – trowel, drowsy, rowdy, towering, coward.

Example words from SME books – VB Textbook Level 2 Page 29 FWP Pages 42-45	power	shower	powerful
	trowel	rowdy	towering
	drowsy	towel	allow
	allowed	powder	coward

Teaching points – Page 40

Point out silent letters.

Vocabulary – guide, vague.

Example words from SME books – VB Textbook Level 2 Page 30 FWP Pages 42-45	often	biscuits	famous	know	wrong
	hour	guard	guests	build	answer
	knew	guy	building	vague	honest
	guide	listen	tongue	guess	

Teaching points – Page 42

Point out silent letters eg fasten, calm, raspberry.

Vocabulary – trance, prance, calf, glanced, advantage.

Example words from SME books – VB Textbook Level 2 Page 31 FWP Pages 46-49	aunty	prance	calm	France	advantage
	trance	half	answer	palm	raspberry
	dance	calf	advancing	glanced	
	demanded	after	fasten	overcast	

Teaching points – Page 42

Discuss each different ending eg take off 'e' and add 'y' – sensible – sensibly.

When a word ends in 'ful' – single 'l', but double the 'll' when adding 'y'.

Example words from SME books – VB Textbook Level 2 Page 32 FWP Pages 46-49	miserable	painful	wonderfully	handle	probable
	suddenly	probably	helpful	trembles	wonderful
	invisible	truthful	family	simple	
	horribly	thankfully	able	sensible	

Teaching points – Page 44

'au' can be 'aw' as in 'daughter' or 'o' as in 'ostrich', particularly with 'Austria' & 'Australia'.
'Daughter' and 'laugh' – same spelling – different sound.
Vocabulary – auction, laundry, haulage.

Example words from SME books – VB Textbook Level 2 Page 33 FWP Pages 50-53	automobile	laundry	faulty	laughed	sausage
	auction	August	Austrian	faultless	sauce
	daughter	because	Australian	autos	
	caught	fault	haulage	cauliflower	

Teaching points – Page 44

With 'sion' end, root word usually ends in 's'.
Contractions – didn't, don't, I'd.
Vocabulary – nervous, anxious, suspicious, discussion, curious, envious, jealous, etc.

Example words from SME books – VB Textbook Level 2 Page 34 FWP Pages 50-53	nervous	serious	delicious	jealous
	anxious	discussion	tremendous	ridiculous
	admission	permission	marvellous	
	suspicious	curious	envious	

Teaching points – Page 46

Point out letters saying their own name.

Example words from SME books – VB Textbook Level 2 Page 35 FWP Pages 50-53	school	island	only	ghost	tomato
	ago	library	tricycle	diamond	noticed
	poster	motor-bike	iron	finally	silent
	notice	bicycle	wind	potato	violin